COLOR FOR YOUR YARD AND GARDEN

COLOR
FOR YOUR YARD
AND GARDEN

by Elda Haring

ILLUSTRATED WITH PHOTOGRAPHS

A Helen Van Pelt Wilson Book

HAWTHORN BOOKS, INC.
PUBLISHERS, NEW YORK

For
Kathleen Bourke,
with appreciation and affection

Acknowledgments

Without the help of two wonderful people this book would never have been written. First, Helen Van Pelt Wilson, my editor, who convinced me that I had the proper qualifications to do such a work. Without her patient counsel in the many problems that arose, her delicious sense of humor, I would have been completely discouraged. Second, my husband, who not only took many of the photographs for this book, but collected and catalogued for me all the other photographs needed. His unfailing good humor, his patience, encouragement, advice, and understanding have meant more than I can adequately express.

My thanks go to the many suppliers of these photographs: our friends Marion and Wilson Scofield and Margaret and Carl Ellis for letting us take photographs in their lovely gardens; our young friends Gordon and Sherrill Clark for taking pictures in our garden; our friends Ruth and Percy Merry and Isabel Zucker for providing much-needed pictures; Molly Adams and George Taloumis, photographers; G. Hampfler, official photographer for Longwood Gardens; Nelson Groffman, of the Franklin Photo Agency; Stecher-Traung-Schmidt Corporation, lithographers; and the All-America Rose Selections.

I am indebted to the following individuals and nurseries for their courteous help: Lulu Brown, of George J. Ball, Inc.; Juanita Akin, of Bodger Seeds, Ltd.; Worth Brown, of Brown's Bulb Ranch; William W. Brown, of W. Atlee Burpee Co.; R. J. Hutton, of The Conard-Pyle Company; Peter deJager, of P. deJager & Sons, Inc.; Edward Fink, of A. B. Morse Company; John Oliver, of Oliver Nurseries; William J. Park, of George W. Park Seed Co., Inc.; Schreiner's Gardens; Stern's Nurseries; and Mrs. Marie Brandstaetter, of The Wayside Gardens Co.

And for their important help with emergency typing, I wish to thank Irene S. Miller and Helen B. Krieg.

E. H.

Greenwich, Connecticut

Contents

Editor's Foreword

COLOR, a wealth of it, that is your first delightful impression of the Haring garden, whether you see it in early April with patches of golden aconites and purple crocus, or the night before frost when the long border glows like an autumn bonfire. The seasonal effects are brilliant because the Harings have planned it so. In spring, daffodils and tulips dominate the scene; in summer, tall blue accents of delphinium separate drifts of pink phlox and white Shasta daisies; the fall picture is vivid with yellow and bronze chrysanthemums, red zinnias, and orange marigolds, all firmly edged with dwarf marigolds and lavender ageratum.

In the last quarter century there has come a new emphasis on color in the home, in cars, and of course in all forms of advertising. In 1925, the bride was pleased with all-taupe carpets, beige wallpaper, and a white kitchen. Today, floor coverings are every hue, crimson wallpaper is not unknown, and kitchens are likely to be pink or yellow. But while the interior decorator has had his way, the gardener has become more and more green-minded and praise of pachysandra and myrtle fills our horticultural journals. Forgotten are the all-pink, all-blue, all-yellow gardens of Gertrude Jekyll. And there is some justification for this: With so little extra help today we incline to the easy way, and perhaps we are less dedicated gardeners.

Not so the Harings. For them, for all who love the sight of a bright panorama, for many retired people now with time to concern themselves again with plants, gardening has become a way of life—healthful and soul-satisfying, with pleasures that can be shared. The Harings delight in offering great pails of colorful cut flowers to their friends, sick or well. Their church is kept supplied with altar flowers, and come fall, Walter Haring's harvest of dried flowers and foliage is made into arrangements to decorate many a winter living room and dining room, including mine.

Pachysandra and myrtle, worthy as they are, produce no such joy of giving or receiving. It is the plants grown for color which do that. They are grown not only in the beds and borders of the garden proper but also in blocks where a multitude of seedlings can be set out in orderly rows spaced for the quick cultivator rather than the slow hand. The Harings are enthusiastic about this bounty obtained from the many packs of seed they sow, as Elda explains in *The Complete Book of Growing Plants from Seed,* with its directions for some two hundred different plants. Walter is photographer, as well as indefatigable gardener. His careful card file of blooming dates has helped to make possible the glorious—and continuous—parade of color in the Haring garden.

With the guidance of this new book, whose illustrations indicate the brilliant possibilities of both familiar and unfamiliar plants—annuals, perennials, bulbs, shrubs, and trees—all of us, whether we plant large or small, in a suburban yard or in a country garden, can also have a riot of color from the last frost of spring to the first frost of fall.

HELEN VAN PELT WILSON

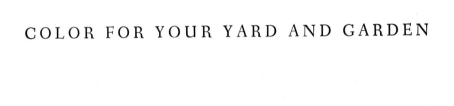

COLOR FOR YOUR YARD AND GARDEN

1

The Excitement of Color

CAN you recapture as I do the response to color that you experience after a long winter when you first enter the main hall of a spring flower show? True, there are other senses involved—nostalgic memories of last year's garden, the overpowering fragrance of hyacinths and herbs, and the musky odor of damp earth—but is not the color spectacle the major attraction? Such experiences, to those of us who enjoy being outdoors and close to nature, are a challenge to make our own yard and garden a harmony of form and color. The plants you choose will inevitably express your personality, judgment, and taste, and the only sincere beginning is to plan for a color scheme that *you* want, regardless of any conventions. The problem then is to find the plants that will grow well together and agreeably build up the desired effect. The fun is to gradually modify, refine, or intensify the combinations and arrangements until you have an individual place of character and charm.

My own flower border has huge masses of bold color: gold and scarlet, deep rose and coral or salmon, rich blues and lavenders, separated and toned down by white flowers or gray foliage. This is my personal feeling for color. Many of my friends find it beautiful; others are unhappy with the combinations I have chosen, just as I cannot appreciate the contrast of dark red tulips with deep purple anemones that appears so often in old Flemish paintings. Some people have a passion for one particular color and prefer a monochrome garden. The challenge is just as great and the results as rewarding. A one-color garden can be most attractive if due consideration has been given to the tones and tints of that color, their juxtaposition, and the provision of varied textures and forms to prevent monotony. A green-and-white garden is usually cool and serene, although it generally makes me want to add a touch of pale pink or yellow for contrast.

With careful selection the smallest garden can contain some color from early spring until late fall. In *New Perennials Preferred*, Helen Van Pelt Wilson describes a narrow strip under her kitchen casement windows. Barely fifteen feet long and two feet wide it has some flowers in bloom from late winter to frost. This is the way she describes it: "You see just under the kitchen casements a length of late-winter-into-summer color from bulbs, perennials, evergreen shrubs—a dwarf ilex at one corner, a fragrant daphne at the other—and the pink spring mountain clematis at the end. Winter iris, the very earliest crocus in purple and yellow, are followed by a few plants of nasturtiums so perfect for kitchen bouquets. Dutch iris 'Golden Harvest' and yellow or apricot violas . . . all these make the kitchen door a spot worth passing by."

When we began to garden years ago and were completely inexperienced, we studied books and pored over the charts and planting hints in nursery and seed catalogues. If our budget was limited, our determination was boundless. Over the years we made many mistakes, and we still experience failures, since the vagaries of climate and weather frequently thwart our best efforts. In a cold season, flowering will be later than expected, and in an unduly hot period it is premature, so that occasionally plants that we had planned to bloom in sequence all burst forth together.

Although our first garden was very small, shrubs and flowering trees provided color from spring to autumn. There was adequate lawn space to accommodate a dogwood and a flowering crab, and along the back line of the yard we planted other flowering shrubs. Nanking cherry (*Prunus tomentosa*), forsythia, weigela, and mock-orange, set out in groups, created a handsome effect. Along the side boundary, mountain-ash, shadbush, and viburnum were showy not only in their flowers but in their autumn fruits.

Daffodils and tulips were planted under the trees. At the feet of deciduous shrubs were drifts of snowdrops, winter aconites, and grape-hyacinths. Scillas and chionodoxas were tucked into every available spot. Clumps of yellow, white, and lavender crocus were set where we could enjoy their early bloom from the kitchen and dining-room windows.

Our twenty-foot-long perennial garden was filled with color from spring until real frost. To achieve it we had spent many hours making plans on graph paper, listing plants by their height and blooming season. On the layouts, groups of plants that flower at the same time alternated with others that bloom later. We relied on the gray foliage of artemisia, santolina, and other dusty millers to separate clashing colors. Accents were made with gladiolus, dahlia, and Peruvian daffodil. Although not many plants could be accommodated in so small a garden, there was always color to be enjoyed. We used annuals for edging and to fill in the gaps between shrubbery in foundation plantings. We had yet to learn the possibilities of color contrast in the winter months by means of broad-leaved evergreens and the delightful hellebores.

When planning your color panorama, let flowering trees be your first consideration. They are many and varied. Early bloomers such as magnolia can be used with early daffodils and tulips. Flowering crab apples, plums, and cherries can be underplanted with midseason tulips or small bulbs. The few summer-flowering trees such as albizzia and gordonia can be planted to blend with any garden picture. The same is true of flowering shrubs, beginning in early spring with the French pussy willow and cornelian cherry. Forsythia follows, blooming with the first daffodils and tulips. As the season advances, we have azaleas, lilacs, bridal wreath, deutzia, rhododendrons, weigela, and mock-orange. Midsummer has the blue spikes of the chaste-tree, the pink, lavendar, or white flowers of rose-of-Sharon, and the fluffy pink spires of tamarix.

The next salient group of plants to include in your color scheme is the perennials. A number of them are extremely long-lived. Their winter-dormant roots respond readily to the first mild days of late winter and may show active growth in very early spring. Late April and May bring the blooms of arabis, basket-of-gold, doronicum, perennial candytuft, primula, forget-me-not, and many others. As they fade, columbine, peony, and iris take over; then come delphiniums, Shasta daisies, and daylilies. Soon the true lilies enliven the garden with their brilliance and fragrance. Phlox, veronica, monarda, and physostegia stage their show in mid-to-late summer. In early autumn the heleniums, Michaelmas daisies, and chrysanthemums provide warm rich colors.

And now the annuals, so clear and bright and sparkling that I cannot imagine a garden without them. Hybridizers have created an unlimited range of colors in the flowers of annuals. This and their great variety of height, habit, form, and foliage make them enormously valuable for quick and interesting effects in many parts of the garden. They are often used as one or several kinds in beds and narrow borders; to cover unforeseen bare spaces; to screen unsightly yellowing foliage (which should not be removed) of bulbs, Oriental poppies, and bleeding-hearts; and to combine with perennials in the hardy border. For people who are occupying a place only for a season or two, annuals can supply a maximum of color at minimum cost.

The tender bulbs, corms, and tubers—gladiolus, ismene, dahlia, acidanthera, and others pictured in this book—should not be overlooked in planning the garden. Some of them are unusual and dramatic and can contribute a different quality of foliage and flower.

Our many years of gardening and our present over-large garden have been the source of most of the cultural information in the accompanying text. Many of the photographs were taken in our own gardens. Plants of most of the species and varieties shown are available by mail order or from local nurseries. Many also, particularly the annuals and perennials, can be easily grown from seed, the most economical and exciting way.

It is my fervent hope that this book will persuade you to explore farther in the territory which it partly covers. My aim has been to tempt you with pictures, to supply the essentials of cultivation and care, and to suggest a few of the very many possible combinations and effects which can bring our gardens closer to the ideal.

2

The Colors of Flowers, Fruits, and Leaves

The author in her golden garden. Walter Haring photo.

YELLOW TO ORANGE

Yellow is the herald of spring, the companion of the summer sun, and the featured player in autumn's pageant. Varieties of yellow-to-bronze flowers are myriad and because of their compatibility with other colors can be used in almost any landscape or garden scene. Either in specimen plants or in a mixed border, brilliant yellow is made more brilliant by sunlight and on dark and cheerless days still gives out some of its warmth and brightness.

Fortunately, yellow flowers are more plentiful than any others, for pale yellow is as important for dividing strong colors as are white and green. An entire garden of yellow hues graduating from subtle creams and pale tones through gold and orange, to almost incandescent flame, and then into the citrons and tawny shades, can provide many interesting garden pictures throughout the entire growing season.

ACHILLEA *filipendulina*
fernleaf yarrow   3 to 4 feet

PERENNIAL.   These are strong, erect plants with finely cut, soft, downy leaves. The individual flowers are small, compactly set in stiff, flat heads from 2½ to 4 inches across, lemon-to-golden yellow. Some consider the plants coarse, but they provide vivid color and are probably best used as accents. The June-to-August flowers last well when cut and keep their color when dried for winter bouquets. Achillea is easily grown, dependable in full sun, preferring dry places; it may need staking. Divide every three or four years. This contrasts brilliantly with delphinium, globe-thistle, speedwell, and blue salvia, and blends with Shasta daisies and butterfly-weed. A large crock or jar filled with cut achillea is stunning on terrace or patio. The Wayside Gardens Co. photo

ALLIUM   6 inches to 5 feet

BULB.   Alliums comprise a large group. The onion is one species. Garden alliums have showy flowers often in spherical heads on thick stems. Some of the lower growers among them are suitable for the rock garden; the taller kinds for the border. Plant in early fall in good garden soil and in full sun. Most alliums bloom in June or July. *A. karataviense* has broad, lustrous, blue-gray leaves, and the plant is lovely even without the 3-inch white flower-heads. *A. caeruleum* bears blue flowers on stems 18 to 24 inches long. *A. moly* (illustrated) has clustered starlike yellow flowers in late May or June. Most spectacular is *A. giganteum*, with 6-inch globes of rosy lilac on 5-foot stems, also in June. Walter Haring photo

ALSTROEMERIA *aurantiaca*
    Peruvian-lily   2 to 4 feet

RHIZOMATOUS PERENNIAL. These showy yet exquisite plants (from Chile rather than Peru) are not reliably hardy north of Washington, D.C., though with protection they have survived in some gardens farther north, especially near the sea. Leafy stems in late June bear umbels of many flowers like small lilies. *A. aurantiaca* is yellow, spotted with brown; *A. ligtu* is pink, white, or lilac. Light rich soil in a sunny or semi-shaded (if warm) situation is best. Because the roots are extraordinarily brittle and tangled, great care is needed in transplanting. Also, stems tend to be weak; a support of twigs or slender canes is desirable. In the North, plant in spring when danger of frost is past, and in the fall lift very carefully and store in damp sand in a cool cellar. In the South, plant in fall. And wherever wintered out of doors, mulch heavily with leaves or straw. In spring, separate the mulch around the new stems and leave it to keep the earth cool above the delicate roots. These plants are well worth any amount of care. Their flowers continue to open for five weeks. In conjunction with regal lilies or some hybrid lilies they give a brilliant effect. Paul E. Genereux photo

ALYSSUM *saxatile*
basket-of-gold   1 to 1½ feet

PERENNIAL. Wide-spreading mats of gray-green foliage are profusely covered with golden to sulphur-yellow flowers in late April or May. *Compactum* is the best form for edging; variety *citrinum* (illustrated) is less strident, a more pleasing shade. Either is delightful when billowing over a slope, a dry wall, or a boulder in the rock garden. Rich soil is needed, but it should never be heavy or over-damp. Avoid wet pockets or low ground. These are long-lived, prolific plants in sun or light shade but they can be killed by below-zero weather without snow-cover. Early forget-me-nots, pansies, dwarf iris, scillas, and lavender or maroon tulips are good neighbors. The Wayside Gardens Co. photo

ANTHEMIS *tinctoria*
camomile, marguerite   2 to 3 feet

PERENNIAL. A favorite of gardeners for centuries, this has deeply divided leaves and flower-heads to 2 inches across of rather short yellow rays with a darker yellow disk. Anthemis blooms profusely from June to September. It is not particular about soil, grows well in dry locations, and like most daisies lasts for many days in bouquets. It is well placed with blue veronica, campanula, delphinium, and blue flax. Walter Haring photo

AQUILEGIA
columbine   1½ to 2 feet

PERENNIAL. Modern garden columbines are mostly superb hybrids that yet retain something of the airy grace of the wild species. From clumps of light green, three-lobed leaves rise numerous wiry stems branching toward the top. From each branch in late May and June hang one or several delicate flowers. The species *A. chrysantha* (right) has all-yellow flowers, the sepals somewhat paler. The Mrs. Scott Elliott and McKana Giant Hybrids (above) include a wide range of colors—pink, rose-red, or lavender—the spurs frequently yellow or white. Plant in full sun or thin shade, in rich light soil. Though quite hardy, columbines are not long-lived but do self-sow readily. New plants should be kept coming from spring-sown seed. Iris is the ideal complement, the foliage and the flowers of both plants contrasting and harmonizing perfectly. A. B. Morse Company photo

ARGEMONE *grandiflora*
  prickly-poppy   2½ to 3 feet

ANNUAL. This is considered a pernicious weed in warm climates but is often grown as a delightful annual in gardens in the North. The foliage is gray-green and rough, the attractive cup-shaped flowers yellow, lavender, or white, from July to frost. Plants make good accents in mixed borders or flower beds, and are at their best in hot, dry locations. Plant near *Salvia farinacea* or bachelor's-buttons for color contrast; near snapdragons for contrast of texture and form. Walter Haring photo

ASCLEPIAS *tuberosa*
  butterfly-weed   2 feet

PERENNIAL. A member of the milkweed family, this American wildflower can be a brilliant and vigorous garden plant. Foliage is green with a golden tinge. The orange flowers, sometimes tipped with red, are carried in umbels and open from July to September. They are an unfailing attraction to the big Monarch butterfly. The long, pointed seed-pods are also decorative. Tap-rooted, this plant resents transplanting and is safely moved only with a large root ball. Growth does not show above ground until late May, so mark the location to prevent damage from early cultivation. Grow in average soil and in full sun. Walter Haring photo

CALENDULA *officinalis*
  pot-marigold   18 inches or less

ANNUAL. Deservedly one of the best-known annuals, this can be grown almost anywhere in the country. The bright flowers are useful in beds, in the border, in containers. Leaves are soft green and fuzzy, the thick stems crowned with daisy flowers in tints of yellow, apricot, orange, and cream from July until frost in the North. Forms vary from single to highly compact with seemingly hundreds of petals, like 'Flame Beauty' (illustrated). Some are tipped or streaked bicolors. Some are 3 inches across. In the Deep South calendulas are valued for winter bloom, but they resent high heat and, where summers are very warm, are best planted in June for fall bloom. Any good soil suits calendulas, as long as they are well watered in dry weather. They combine well with stokesia, ageratum, cornflowers, and snapdragons.

A good foil for the warm-colored varieties is snow-on-the-mountain. Bodger Seeds, Ltd., photo

CALLIOPSIS *tinctoria*   9 to 18 inches

ANNUAL. These gay plants are actually various annual species and their hybrids of coreopsis. Daisy flowers, single or double, in yellow, orange, and red, are held above ferny or sometimes threadlike foliage. Many have zones of contrasting color, or are striped or marbled. 'Golden Crown' and 'Golden Ray' are clear yellow with dark red or maroon centers. Others have red petals, sometimes touched with gold. Seed sown in May will yield bloom from mid-July on. They also seed themselves. Grow in any soil, in full sun. A planting in mixed colors is well set off by white petunias, white veronicas, or snapdragons. Verbenas, with their dark leaves, make good neighbors, or anchusa 'Bluebird.' W. Atlee Burpee Co. photo

13

CALTHA *palustris*
    marsh-marigold   1 foot

PERENNIAL. As the name implies, this wildflower always frequents very wet places. From Newfoundland to South Carolina and in the Middle West it is one of the cherished signatures of spring. Each plant forms a bold clump of bright green, rounded leaves and in late March or early April produces quantities of somewhat fleshy buttercup flowers an inch to 2 inches across. Later the leaves become very large and by midsummer are unsightly. By that time, in the woods, overhanging shrubs such as spice-bush and alder, and the fronds of royal or ostrich ferns virtually hide the marigold foliage. A similar association can be followed in the wild garden. Rich woodsy soil and abundant moisture are obviously essential, and preferably the very margin of a brook or pond. Walter Haring photo

CAMPSIS *radicans*
    trumpet-vine   25 feet

VINE. This hardy climber has long sprays of decorative compound leaves and in late summer bears clusters of large flowers, tubular with five spreading lobes, the tube yellow to orange, the lobes pink to deep orange. It climbs by aerial rootlets, fastening itself to brick, stone, or wood and is a rapid grower for covering porches and walls. It makes a charming picture clambering through an old tree—to which it does no harm. Plant in full sun in soil not over-rich. A. B. Morse Company photo

CENTAUREA *macrocephala*
  globe- or golden centaurea   3 feet

PERENNIAL. Coarse-leaved and stiff-stemmed, this plant is hardly graceful, but it is most effective and useful with its large thistle flowers of brilliant gold in July. Excellent in the mixed border and a favorite of butterflies. The spherical involucre that holds the petals dries beautifully for winter bouquets. Plant in full sun in average soil. Shasta daisies, balloon-flower, and globe-thistle provide pleasing contrasts; the deeper orange or maroon daylilies offer good related colors. *C. gymnocarpa*, a hardy plant to 2 feet high, is grown for its white-woolly, much-divided leaves. It is one of several plants called dusty miller. Walter Haring photo

CHEIRANTHUS *allioni*
  wallflower   1 to 2 feet

PERENNIAL OR BIENNIAL. Although wallflowers can be perennial in areas of mild winters, in the North they are of doubtful hardiness, unless grown in a protected garden. The fragrant orange or golden flowers are borne in dense clusters over crowns of gray-green foliage in May. *C. allioni* if sown indoors in February will bloom in late summer. If sown in June, the small plants can be wintered over to bloom the next May. The new 'Apricot Delight' (illustrated) is biennial, blooming the second season from spring-sown seed and does not need winter protection. *C. kewensis*, brownish orange, is hardy only where winters are practically frost-free. Plant in full sun in rich garden soil. George W. Park Seed Co., Inc., photo

CHRYSANTHEMUM

(garden hybrids)   1 to 4 feet

PERENNIAL. There are chrysanthemums for every situation—low, medium, and tall —early, midseason, and late, and some that bloom for weeks. No other flower creates such positive color and warmth in the au- tumn garden. Some kinds make compact cushions of rather small flowers, others are open and spreading, with loosely double flowers to 2½ inches across. There are but- ton flowers, and those with the rays nar- row, inrolled, spidery, or spoon-shaped. There are endless gradations of tone, from

brilliant to muted, in every color but blue. Pungent foliage, hardiness, and the habit of increasing each year combine to make chrysanthemums one of the most satisfactory of garden plants.

Plant in full sun in soil improved with peatmoss and bonemeal. Fertilize once a month with 5-10-5 fertilizer and water deeply every ten days unless there is heavy rainfall. Maintain a mulch of peatmoss or salt hay. Pinch out the tops when 6 inches high to encourage branching. For large individual flowers, pinch off the side buds as soon as they are visible but don't disbud the spray types. In the third year lift and divide the clumps. Molly Adams photo

C. *carinatum*
summer chrysanthemum   1½ feet

ANNUAL. Attractive, crisp, and clean-cut daisy flowers (below) come in shades of yellow and white, brown, pink, rose, and lavender, and are sometimes tipped with brown or black—gay when used in a mixture. This is an excellent summer annual where the climate is exceptionally cool, or it can be grown in frost-free areas for winter bloom. Solid beds of annual chrysanthemums bordered by ageratum or lobelia are striking. In the North, seed should be sown indoors in March to provide a long blooming season. W. Atlee Burpee Co. photo

CHRYSOGONUM *virginianum*
green-and-gold   1 foot

PERENNIAL. A wildflower that often carpets the foothills of the Piedmont and Blue Ridge Ranges, this should be more widely grown in gardens, for it is very hardy, makes thick spreading patches of olive-green leaves, and is covered from May to July with golden 1½-inch stars, a bright and charming plant. Woods soil and semi-shade in the rockery or on the edge of a wild garden or shrub border is a suitable situation. A top-dressing of leafmold in autumn is recommended. In the southeastern states, the leaves are evergreen. *Phlox divaricata,* trillium, and wood ferns make attractive companions. Walter Haring photo

COREOPSIS *grandiflora*
tickseed   2 to 3 feet

PERENNIAL. New Englanders used to call this plant "cut-and-come-again," for no perennial produces more flowers for so long a period, provided the faded ones are removed. The leaves are mostly basal, the stems long, arching, and firm, each tipped by a 2½-inch flower with wide, notched, bright yellow rays. A semidouble form is illustrated. It grows readily in any soil that is not stiff and heavy, and it needs full sun. The sparseness of foliage suggests placing it in small groups, near well-foliaged plants, such as delphinium, hemerocallis, or veronica. W. Atlee Burpee Co. photo

18

CORNUS *mas*
cornelian-cherry   10 feet

SHRUB or SMALL TREE. The cornel of English hedgerows is hardy in American gardens, flowering very early in spring. The habit is branching, and every branch bears little clusters of small, pale yellow, apetalous flowers before the broad-ovate leaves put forth. And in midsummer abundant red fruits appear. It blends well with other shrubs or makes a handsome small specimen tree standing alone. Crocus, drifted across the ground below, will bloom at the same time. A. B. Morse Company photo

CYTISUS *praecox*
Warminster broom   4 to 5 feet

SHRUB. In May this is one of the most spectacular of all shrubs, when it is a fountain of pale yellow pealike flowers. In summer the small light green leaves give it an airy look. Plant in a not-too-rich porous soil in sun. Because the long deep root makes transplanting difficult, it is wise to obtain this broom potted or balled-and-burlapped. In front of dark evergreens or isolated as a specimen it is magnificent, so much so as to need no competing companions. Walter Haring photo

19

CROCUS   4 to 6 inches

BULB. This is one of the most welcome flowers of late winter and early spring. Toward the end of February and beginning of March the large cupped blooms open in the cold. The grassy foliage usually comes later. Of the many species and hybrids, *C. chrysanthus* (below) is one of the finest, with orange-yellow flowers; its va-

riety, 'E. A. Bowles', is a softer yellow. The earliest to bloom in the Northeast is *C. imperati* (opposite top), lilac or white, with purple stripes. *C. tomasinianus* comes later in March, the silvery buds maturing to lavender or purple, the stigmas bright orange. 'Purity' (opposite bottom) is a handsome cultivar. Cheerful when edging a foundation or border or in little colonies in the rockery, the crocus can also be na-

turalized in lawns and woodland, broadcast generously in irregular drifts of one or two kinds with some whites or pale yellows among deeper colors. Plant in rich soil in sun and let the foliage remain (and this can be a nuisance in a lawn) until it has turned yellow; otherwise the bulbs will soon "run out." Walter Haring (*Chrysanthus* and 'Purity') and P. deJager & Sons, Inc., photos

DAHLIA 15 inches to 5 feet

TUBER. In the mountains of Mexico and Guatemala the dahlia grows as a wild plant. From two species brought to Europe at the end of the eighteenth century have come virtually all of the magnificent kinds of today. There are dwarf, medium high, and very tall ones. The flowers come in all colors and combination of colors except true blue and are single, semidouble, and double in compact formal heads, little pompons, or massive sunbursts up to 12 inches across, the petals blunt or pointed (as in these cactus hybrids), flat, convex, or quilled. Stems are strong, the foliage bold. The blooming period is from mid-July until frost for the lower-growing kinds, from late summer to frost for the tall ones

In spring after all danger of frost, make plantings in full sun and in soil rich in organic matter, such as peatmoss or leafmold. For each tuber prepare a planting hole 8 inches deep and wide, insert a strong stake, and leave a basin to be filled with soil as the plant grows. Feeding and frequent watering are important.

The dwarf dahlias may be used as annuals and grown from seed sown outdoors in May where plants are to stay, or sown earlier indoors in March. They need not be staked. Coltness and Unwin Hybrids are excellent for bedding. 'Fall Festival' and 'Zulu', with dark-red finely cut foliage and red flowers, make handsome accents through the perennial border. George W. Park Seed Co., Inc., photo

DORONICUM *clusi*

leopard's-bane   1½ to 3 feet

PERENNIAL. This excellent plant for the border starts to bloom in late April and continues for several weeks. Quantities of long-stemmed golden daisy flowers rise 2 feet from a crown of handsome leaves. *D. plantagineum* produces extra large flowers on 3-foot stems and blooms a little later and longer than *D. clusi*. Both species will grow in average soil in sun or part shade. In some areas plants go dormant and disappear in July or August, so their location should be well marked. Bleeding-hearts, Virginia bluebells, and narcissus are lovely neighbors. The Wayside Gardens Co. photo

ERANTHIS *hyemalis*

winter aconite   6 to 8 inches

TUBEROUS. In late February, in sheltered places, in March where more exposed, this is probably the very first flower to show in northern gardens. Its yellow-satin cups, 1½ inches across, are surrounded by a collar of notched leaves. Winter-hardy and long-lived, it also self-sows and spreads where soil and site are to its liking: a well-drained humus soil in a place where trees will later provide some shade. Thus it will thrive as a ground-cover in open woods. Set it out in autumn in drifts with snowdrops for a lovely late-winter picture. Walter Haring photo

ERYTHRONIUM
trout-lily, dogtooth-violet   10 inches

BULB. Among the earliest of spring flowers, the trout-lilies are particularly suited to the wild garden and for massing under deciduous trees and shrubs. The lilylike flowers are borne on slender stems on narrow, spotted foliage. Different varieties have delicate colors and tints of white, cream, yellow, or rose. They are forest or mountain plants, needing shade or semishade and rich, woodsy soil. Plant the bulbs 2 inches deep in the fall, and supply a light protective mulch in winter. They increase readily over the years if not disturbed by cultivation. Each plant has only two leaves, most essential for the growth of new bulbs, so they should never be picked, though the flowers may be. George W. Park Seed Co., Inc., photo

ESCHSCHOLTZIA *californica*
California poppy   8 to 15 inches

ANNUAL. A rampant perennial in the frost-free Southwest, this is grown as a more controlled annual in the North. It is excellent for overplanting tulip bulbs and good in the rock garden, where it blooms all summer. The airy foliage is blue-gray, the open cup-shaped flowers yellow, orange, cream, rose, or scarlet. For earliest bloom, sow seed late in fall where plants are to grow or lightly scratch in seed around bulb foliage in April, and blooms will then open from July to frost. Plant in average soil in full sun. The California poppy is wonderfully drought-resistant. Ageratum, lobelia, and salvia 'Blue Bedder' are good adjacent plants. W. Atlee Burpee Co. photo

FORSYTHIA
goldenbells   4 to 8 feet

SHRUB. In April how many dreary places are suddenly transformed by the presence of even one bush of the familiar forsythia? Graceful, hardy, long-lived, and disease-free, what garden can do without it? The foliage is attractive all summer and fall. To grow it well, give it deep soil and plenty of sun and water, and every year or two prune out some of the thick woody canes of old wood from the base, for it blooms on the arching new stems. *F. suspensa* is good for covering banks because the branches bend down and tip-root, though it does not bloom well in the extreme North, where *F. obovata* will dependably do so. *F. spectabilis* (illustrated) is the showiest and most commonly seen species.

It and *F. intermedia*, with lighter yellow blooms, and the hybrid 'Beatrice Farrand', with very large flowers, are most satisfactory and easy to grow. Walter Haring photo

GAZANIA
African daisy   1 to 1½ feet

ANNUAL. Coming from South Africa, where it is usually perennial, gazania is drought-resistant and one of the showiest low-growing plants. For our country, it is treated as an annual. In frost-free areas, it can be grown for winter flowers. For earliest blooms in the North, sow seed indoors in March. In May, set out plants in good garden soil in sun. The flowers are held on tall stems well above green rosettes of foliage, and the colors are a bright medley of cream, yellow, gold, orange, rose, and red. 'Fire Emerald' offers a colorful mixture of flowers 3 inches or more across, and the plants are robust. Gazanias make excellent ground-covers and bedding plants. George W. Park Seed Co., Inc., photo

HELENIUM
Helen's-flower   2½ to 4 feet

PERENNIAL. These old-time dependable plants have again come into vogue, the modern hybrids being far superior to the species. They bloom profusely for six to eight weeks from August on, when most other perennials are ripening seeds. Daisy flowers, 1½ to 2½ inches across, in yellow, tawny orange, copper, or red-brown surmount sturdy branching stems. Plant in any good soil, in sun. When clumps become overgrown, they can be divided in spring for extra plants. Fine varieties are 'Brilliant', a tapestry of autumn color, 'Moerheim Beauty', velvety brown-red, and 'Riverton Gem', gold-to-red. White phlox, white snakeroot (*Eupatorium rugosum*), Michaelmas daisies, and hardy ageratum (*Eupatorium coelestinum*) blend with heleniums. Walter Haring photo

HELIANTHUS
sunflower   15 inches to 8 feet

ANNUAL. The familiar species, *H. giganteus*, grows too tall and bold for the small yard or garden. More suitable are 'Sungold' to 6 feet and 'Teddy Bear' to 3 feet, both covered with 4-inch, double, yellow or gold flowers on thick shrubby foliage. 'Italian White' has lighter, more airy foliage and is covered all summer with long-stemmed, single flowers in white or cream. Sunflowers must bask in the warmth of the sun, but are not particular about soil. The tall ones are good in borders and attractive as temporary hedges or screens in the summer garden. Walter Haring photo

HELICHRYSUM *bracteatum*
strawflower   3 feet

ANNUAL. The famous "immortelle" of European gardens is usually seen as a bedding plant where summers are hot and dry, but it is even better known in dried winter bouquets. From July until frost long-stemmed daisy flowers in shades of yellow, orange, pink, rose, also white, often very double, are borne in profusion. A light, warm soil is best. In the North, sow seeds indoors in March, for these plants need a long growing season. For dried flowers, cut them in the bud stage and hang in bunches upside-down in a dry place. The colors hold for months. W. Atlee Burpee Co. photo

HELIOPSIS
orange sunflower   2 to 4 feet

PERENNIAL. The native species is too coarse for most gardens but the modern hybrids are excellent. Long, wiry stems make them invaluable for cutting. The habit is branching with many golden daisies, usually double or semidouble, from late June to September. The subtle 'Gold-Greenheart' has a green center; 'Summer Sun' (shown here with pink phlox) will bloom the first year if seed is sown indoors in March. Both are extremely hardy and will live for years. Plant heliopsis in average soil and divide every three or four years. Walter Haring photo

HEMEROCALLIS
daylily   1½ to 5 feet

PERENNIAL. Perhaps the hardiest, most adaptable, and most immune to trouble of all perennials, these plants have grassy leaves and a wealth of trumpet flowers. As the name implies, each flower lasts for only a day, but new buds keep opening for weeks. Some varieties bloom at night and are nice to grow in a tub on a balcony or terrace. Although the old *H. flava* and 'Hyperion' are still enjoyed, a multitude of hybrids are now available in clear tones of yellow, cream, orange, pink, red, and off-colors of apricot, copper, and mahogany. The carefree daylilies are undemanding as to soil. But do give them at least six hours of sun, and apply 5-10-5 fertilizer every spring. Along the edges of meadows and woods, you may find them escaped or naturalized. In the perennial border they harmonize with most garden flowers. They are also effective planted alone in borders along walks or driveways.

Shown above are daylilies in the author's garden, Walter Haring photo, and below, in the Percy Merry garden. On facing page: above left, 'Irene Nehring'; above right, 'Floral Pattern'; center left, 'Merrywill'; center right, 'Finlandia'; bottom, 'Star Ruby'—all from The Merrys Nursery. Percy Merry photos

HUNNEMANNIA *fumariaefolia*
Mexican tulip-poppy   1½ feet

ANNUAL. This lovely poppy is perennial in the Lower South but must be grown as an annual farther north. The foliage is feathery, bluish green, and disease-free. Satiny cup-shaped flowers, 2 to 3 inches across, are borne on long stems excellent for cutting. Sow seed in May where the plants are to grow, in well-drained soil and full sun. Germination may take as much as three weeks. As poppies resent transplanting, sow thickly and thin the seedlings to 10 inches apart for a bedding effect. They will bloom from mid-July until frost. With blue salvia or salpiglossis as a background and with purple or lavender petunias in front, you can create a memorable effect. Walter Haring photo

HYACINTHUS
hyacinth   8 to 18 inches

BULB. This fragrant, early spring-blooming flower has been cultivated for centuries. The florets grow evenly around the stem, resulting in flower spikes that are beautiful from every side. Flowers are yellow, as here, also pink, rose, lavender, white, and blue. They are often used in formal beds but are more delightful when planted individually or in clusters for color under trees and shrubs or in long drifts. Plant hyacinths in October or November, 6 inches deep and 6 inches apart in rich garden soil. Then they will last for years. Walter Haring photo

HYPERICUM
St. John's-wort   1 to 2 feet

SHRUB. Throughout the summer, hypericum bears bright yellow flowers about an inch across. The seed-pods that follow are the favorite food of goldfinches in winter. The low-growing *H. calycinum* (illustrated) and 'Hidcote' are best for the rock garden or as ground-covers. The taller 'Sungold', with larger flowers, has proved hardier than the others in normally colder areas. Plant in light, well-drained soil in sun or part shade. The Wayside Gardens Co. photo

KNIPHOFIA
tritoma, torch-lily   3 feet

PERENNIAL. Sometimes also called red-hot poker, this plant produces spikes of bloom from June or early July until frost. Some kinds have all-yellow, coral, or orange flowers, in other kinds the lower, opened flowers are white or yellow, the upper ones in the bud stage, coral or scarlet. In the North, the roots must be dug in late autumn and transferred to a covered coldframe for the winter, or stored indoors like cannas. Plant tritomas 4 inches deep in rich well-drained soil in sun; provide plenty of moisture during dry weather. The rather coarse grassy foliage makes them useful as accents or in groups by themselves. They are effective with globe-thistle and Michaelmas daisies. George W. Park Seed Co., Inc., photo

31

LABURNUM *vossi*

goldenchain-tree   30 feet

TREE. This is a beautiful flowering tree for late May or early June. At first somewhat shrubby, it grows into an excellent specimen tree. It is also good for light shade near a house, in the background of the garden or in woodland. Long tapering racemes of yellow pea-flowers contrast with delicate gray-green foliage; the long green seed-pods turn black in autumn and are poisonous. Not reliably hardy in colder areas, it will usually thrive there on the east or south side of a building. Plant in rather rich soil. The Wayside Gardens Co. photo

LILIUM
lily   1½ to 5 feet

BULB. Lilies are universally loved for the stately beauty that gives character and quality to any garden. Heights, forms, and colors vary with species and variety. For late May and early June there are the Rainbow and Bellingham Hybrids in shades of yellow, gold, orange, red, pink. In late June are the Mid-Century Hybrids, with vivid, up-facing flowers, two of which, 'Cinnabar' and 'Croesus', are shown below left. The white *L. regale* (right) and *L. candidum* (Madonna lily) bloom in June. For midseason there are the Fiesta Hybrids and Turk's-cap lilies followed by the Aurelian and Olympic Hybrids. In late August and September the Oriental Hybrids and *L. speciosum, L. auratum,* and its variety *rubrum* bring deep color to the border.

Bulbs will rot in constantly moist or heavy soils; they need a deep, rich soil that is well drained. Open up heavy clay soils with quantities of peat moss or leafmold turned under with 5-10-5 fertilizer. Plant the small-sized bulbs with 2 to 3 inches of soil cover; medium-sized, 3 to 4 inches; and large ones, 4 to 6 inches. Bulbs of the Madonna lilies, however, are never covered with more than 2 inches of soil. Space all of them 6 inches apart for bedding effect or 10 to 12 inches as accent plants. Maintain a deep mulch to keep roots cool. In the border, coralbells, nepeta, balloon-flower, delphinium, and blue iris go well with the early lilies. Photos: Mid-Century Hybrids, Oregon Bulb Farms, Herman V. Wall; *L. regale,* Walter Haring.

LONICERA
  honeysuckle   6 to 20 feet

VINE. Scenting the air for yards around, Hall's honeysuckle, *L. japonica halliana* (illustrated), grows rampantly in sun or shade in almost any soil. It is much used for ground-covers, especially on banks, and is delightful near a porch in the evening. A favorite for over a century, it can become a pest if allowed to encroach on fine shrubs or trees. The flowers change from white to yellow. *L. heckrotti* climbs to 10 feet, is more controlled, hardy, and ever-blooming, its rose-and-yellow flowers fragrant only at night; *L. henryi* closely resembles Hall's honeysuckle but grows more slowly and does not get out of bounds. The last two species are evergreen where winters are mild and semi-evergreen farther north. The Wayside Gardens Co. photo

NARCISSUS
daffodil   10 to 20 inches

BULB. The great number of named varieties of narcissus testifies to the popularity of this bulb. Shown here are (above) 'Preamble', 'Slieveboy', 'Empress of Ireland'; (center) the small 'February Gold'; (below) 'Sun Chariot', 'Sleveen', and 'Kilworth'. Almost all, even the large-flowered hybrids, have a distinctive purity and wild grace. Added to the wide range of tints of yellow and cream or cold white are bicolors with pink, orange, or orange-edged cups. Some are large trumpets, others shallow cups. Some have multiple flowers on one stalk. There are enchanting diminutives for the rock garden. For all, the soil should contain peatmoss. Plant the bulbs in September as early as you can get them, watering thoroughly afterward. Give them bonemeal in the fall and superphosphate in early spring. And never remove the leaves until they turn yellow; they are needed in the formation of next year's flower. Daffodils combine beautifully with early tulips and grape-hyacinths. In quantity they make wonderful pictures with forsythia, magnolias, and *Spiraea thunbergi*. The white or pink and white varieties are fine with flowering crabapples and cherries. P. deJager & Sons, Inc., photo

NEMESIA *strumosa*

figwort   8 to 12 inches

ANNUAL. Nothing could be more appealing for an edging or to fill a bare space in the rock garden than this little plant with its masses of inch-wide, broad-lipped flowers—yellow, orange, red, pink, rose, or white. Here are shown some plants of the Triumph strain. The very bushy habit is pleasing, and the flowers keep coming all summer. Nemesia dislikes hot, dry weather, but thrives where summers are cool. In southern California it is generally grown for winter bloom. In other areas seed may be sown outdoors in early May for first flowers in July. Little massed beds of it are charming, too, either by itself in mixed but related colors, or with verbena, sweetalyssum, or yellow pansies. George J. Ball, Inc., photo

OENOTHERA *fruticosa*
evening-primrose, sundrops   1 to 2 feet

PERENNIAL. Virtually all the species of this genus are native in North or South America, and a number of them have been developed by nurserymen into most satisfying garden subjects—hardy, dependable, trouble-free. Flowers are borne in terminal clusters, yellow or gold, on straight stems in late June and continue to open for about six weeks. They can provide areas of vivid color near the front of perennial borders. O. *fruticosa* (illustrated) is the best-known, flowering all day, in spite of its name; its variety *youngi* is stockier, with shiny leaves and erect stems. O. *missouriensis* has trailing stems with pale yellow flowers to 4 inches across and is good for either rock garden or border. Oenotheras love lots of strong sun but will also bloom in semishade. A soil on the dry side is preferred. They should be divided every three years. Campanula, delphinium, white sweet-William, yellow monkshood make interesting effects with evening-primroses. In July they are gorgeous with the tawny *Lilium tigrinum*. Walter Haring photo

POTENTILLA *fruticosa*
buttercup-bush   2 to 3 feet

SHRUB. Of the hundreds of species of pontentilla found in many parts of the world, this one is the finest for our gardens, being exceedingly hardy, densely foliaged with ferny leaves, and studded with yellow chalice-shaped flowers all summer. The greatest display is in June. The floriferous 'Sundrop' and 'Sutter's Gold' are appropriate for the rock garden or the front of a border, and will also make a charming little hedge, as they can be pruned. 'Katherine Dykes' is of graceful form with arched branches and paler yellow flowers. Somewhat less hardy but reliable in the New York area with winter covering, is the foot-high, cherry-red P. *nepalensis* 'Miss Willmott'. All kinds like a rather poor limy soil and full sun. Photo courtesy of Stern's Nurseries, Geneva, New York

PRIMULA
primrose   6 to 12 inches

PERENNIAL. For American gardens, primroses are best divided into two types; the
rock-garden or border kinds, and the taller
growing "candelabras," which need a totally
different situation and care. Wordsworth's
flower, the May-blooming cowslip, *P. veris,*
has rosettes of wrinkled leaves and many-
flowered umbels of fragrant yellow, orange,
brownish, or garnet flowers. *Primula acau-
lis,* also called *P. vulgaris,* is similar but has
a solitary flower on each stem and dozens
of bunched stems to a plant. The color
range includes rich blues and violets.
Crosses of these two produced *P. polyantha*
(illustrated), which has excellent foliage
and larger flowers in dense heads, available
in all colors, even light blue. Another species altogether is *P. denticulata,* from the
Himalayas, which holds up a perfect sphere
of lilac, mauve, or white flowers in late
April. All of these primroses like cool shade
and moisture in summer, but comparative
dryness in winter. The soil should be deep,
rich, and acid with a mulch of peatmoss
or pine needles and an application of dried
cow manure in fall. Do not cultivate close
to the crowns, and divide plants every third
year, after they bloom. Primroses thrive in
moist shaded rock gardens and in woodland. All early spring flowers look well
with them but particularly white hyacinths.
A fruit tree in bloom with *P. denticulata*
beneath makes a lovely spring picture.
Primroses also provide charming bouquets.
Walter Haring photo

RANUNCULUS *asiaticus*
Persian buttercup   10 to 14 inches

TUBER. Primarily a florist's flower, like
a small peony in tones of yellow, rose, scarlet, or white, this is a challenge to grow
out of doors. The picture shows the Teco-
late Giants, a fine strain. Not reliably

hardy north of Washington, D. C., ranunculus has survived in some northern gardens when deeply mulched over winter. To be safe, plant new tubers in early spring. They are odd, clawlike objects, and the claws should be set downward, 2 inches deep, in light, rich, well-drained soil and in sun. When leaves have yellowed, the tubers can be lifted, exposed to the air in a dry place for six weeks, then stored like cannas, and kept quite dry until the end of February. Plant them then separately in small pots and water sparingly until green shoots appear and the weather is warm enough to set them out. If you care to go to this much trouble, you will be amply repaid, as the flowers are elegantly formed and gorgeous massed in beds. W. Atlee Burpee Co. photo

ROSA
   rose   2 to 3 feet

Bush. Hybrid Teas 'Golden Prince' (above right) and 'Golden Girl' (right) are welcome newcomers to the family of yellow roses. Buds are shapely and the handsome double 5-inch flowers lightly scented. Foliage is shiny, waxen green on well-branched bushes that grow to moderate height. We have Joseph Pernet, of France, to thank for roses of this hue. It took ten years of effort in crossing thousands of Hybrid Perpetuals with the old Persian Yellow to get the one seed that produced his 'Soleil d'Or', and from that seed are descended all the yellow, orange, flame-blends, and bicolored roses of today. The Conard-Pyle Company photos

RUDBECKIA

coneflower, gloriosa daisy   1½ to 6 feet

PERENNIAL.   The garden coneflowers are improved forms of the familiar black-eyed-Susan *R. hirta* (right) and hybrids with other species, notably *R. laciniata*. Extremely hardy and disease-free, they add greatly to the August and September garden. The big flowers have mounded or cone-shaped centers of brown, dark red, or black, and 2-inch rich yellow or light red rays. A new one, 'Green Eyes' (below), has a clear green cone. Some bear double flowers, as 'Gold Drop', which grows to 2½ feet, 'Goldquelle' (below right), and the well-known but aphis-prone 'Golden-Glow', which grows to 5 or 6 feet. None is exacting about soil, preferring it on the dry side. Michaelmas daisies with their misty lavenders and violets are a nice foil for these glowing flowers. A less hardy type, often called gloriosa daisy, is usually grown as an annual in the North. The foliage is hairy and rather coarse; the long-stalked flowers have gold rays, mahogany-ringed or -tipped, and are sometimes double. Sow seed in spring and thin out later. Shasta daisy, white phlox, cynoglossum, and veronica go well with these flowers. *R. hirta,* Walter Haring photo; 'Green Eyes', George W. Park Seed Co., Inc., photo; 'Goldquelle', The Wayside Gardens Co. photo

TAGETES
marigold   6 inches to 4 feet

ANNUAL. Even the inexperienced gardener can enjoy marigolds, for it takes no
special skill to develop a whole garden
with the different kinds, as here, the low
ones as edging, medium-high, and tall ones
for background. Seed germinates quickly
when sown directly in the garden in May,
and plants practically take care of themselves, blooming in 6 to 8 weeks. The finely
cut foliage is attractive and untroubled by
pests. Flowers continue to come in quantity until late fall—the dwarf marigolds
often blooming until Thanksgiving. With
their warm colors and varied patterns of
gold, lemon, pumpkin, garnet, persimmon,
and velvety browns, they bring cheer to the
frosty weather.

Though now intercrossed and modified,
there are two main types: the tall, erect,
large-flowered "African" marigolds, and the
dwarf, spreading, often single or semidouble "French." Both are actually natives
of Mexico. Good early varieties are 'Tiger',
low and very double, 'Giant Fluffy',
'Brownie Scout', and the Red and Gold
Hybrids. Blooming from midsummer to
frost are 'Crackerjack', 'Hawaii', 'Alaska',
the Climax and Jubilee Series, and many
others. Any good friable soil pleases them
so long as it is in full sun. Thinning out
and transplanting are easy, even for plants
in bud if they are kept watered for several
days.

The dwarf types combine beautifully
with ageratum, *Lobelia erinus*, white or
purple alyssum, and *Nierembergia*; the tall
types with snapdragons, celosia, zinnias,
blue salvia, cynoglossum, and perilla. W.
Atlee Burpee Co. photo

41

THUNBERGIA *alata*
  black-eyed-Susan-vine   5 feet

VINE. This twining plant is perennial in the South, growing tall enough to cover verandas and arbors. In the North it is an annual with a much shorter reach, excellent as a ground-cover for it will creep, or in a hanging basket as it is here. It can also be trained to a fence post or used in window boxes. Flowers are more than an inch across, cream or orange-yellow with dark centers, and plants bloom all summer. Start seed indoors in March and transplant to the garden in May in average soil but in full sun. George W. Park Seed Co., Inc., photo

TITHONIA *rotundifolia*
Mexican sunflower   4 to 6 feet

ANNUAL. This tall and vigorous plant has deeply lobed, velvety green leaves and 3-inch flowers of luminous orange. Contrary to the common name, blooms are more like orange-red single dahlias than sunflowers. Strong stems make them fine for cutting. 'Torch', growing to 4 feet, and 'Avalon', growing to 8 feet, produce gorgeous flowers from July to frost. Tithonia develops rapidly into a very bushy plant really too bold for the mixed border but wonderful by itself as a screen or background. Rather poor soil in full sun suits it best, and drought does not faze it except in very hot weather. Staking is advisable. Sow the seed in May where plants are to grow, or sow several weeks earlier indoors and transplant. Walter Haring photo

TULIPA
tulip   6 inches to 3 feet

BULB. For masses of color in the spring garden, tulips predominate, at least until mid or late May when the iris holds equal prominence. Our tall tulips are highly developed hybrids from wild Turkish and Persian plants and are often classified in groups though today the groups intergrade. The sturdy Early Dutch tulips have large flowers of usually vivid solid colors on rather short stems. They are best suited to formal beds or neat edgings, perhaps with pansies or early forget-me-nots. Typical are 'Kaiserskroon', scarlet, edged yellow; 'De Wet', orange and salmon; 'Peach Blossom', double; and 'Maréchal Neil', canary. Another early favorite, of a different character, and about 18 inches high, is 'Red Emperor', with giant flowers. Then follow the taller and more graceful Darwin, Greigi, and Triumph tulips in all colors except blue. Latest are the Rembrandt and Cottage tulips, the former having flowers of rich broken-color, often marbled, feathered, or streaked, the latter much like the Darwins. There are scores of varieties differing in flower shape as well as color —wineglass, reflexed, narrow-pointed, wide-spreading, etc. These midseason and late tulips are unrivaled when closely planted in groups of 100 or more of one variety, and lovely in patches of 25 to 50 in the border.

Quite different are the low-growing smaller-flowered kinds classified for convenience as "species" tulips because they are essentially unchanged from tulips still growing wild in parts of the world. They belong more to the rock garden or informal plantings, and are increasingly popular.

Tulipa acuminata, with slender long-tapering orange and yellow petals; *T. clusiana,* cherry-red and white; *T. dasystemon,* starry gold and white, very early; *T. kaufmanniana,* the waterlily tulip; and *T. marjoletti,* palest yellow edged carmine, are among the best known.

Plant tulips in a sunny position in enriched well-drained soil, or in semishade under deciduous trees and shrubs. Plant in late fall in the North and from December to January in the South. A light winter mulch is helpful in colder areas. After tulips have finished flowering, remove the stems but let all the leaves mature until yellowed. This is essential for the growth of the bulb. Tulips benefit by a feeding as they are coming into bloom. In the fall use a 5-10-5 fertilizer or a top-dressing of dried manure and bonemeal. Leave the bulbs in the ground for several seasons then replace them with new bulbs. Tulips combine beautifully with all spring-flowering trees and shrubs, and with perennials such as *Phlox subulata, Alyssum saxatile,* iberis, arabis, and forget-me-nots.

Modern cultivars of "species" tulips: 'Summit' (upper left), 'Pinkeen' (upper right), 'Rondo' (lower left), P. deJager and Sons, Inc., photos; and *Tulipa tarda,* Walter Haring photo

ZANTEDESCHIA *elliottiana*
calla-lily   2 to 3 feet

RHIZOME.   Sometimes offered as *Richardia* or arum-lily, calla-lilies are tender plants much grown in Southern California and other frost-free areas, such as the Pacific Northwest, where they remain in gardens throughout the year. The leaves are arrow-shaped, quite large, dark green, sometimes white-spotted. The flowers of this species are rich yellow, of Z. *aethiopica* white, and of Z. *rehmanni* rose or red. Plant rhizomes 4 to 5 inches deep in a partly sunny location in rich, moist loam. In the North, start them indoors in March or April or set them directly in the garden in late May. Lift and store them over winter in plastic bags in a cool but frost-free place. Brown's Bulb Ranch photo

ZINNIA   1 to 4 feet

ANNUAL. Zinnias are without a doubt the most popular annual grown today. They come fast from seed sown where plants are to grow—in May in the North, in April farther south. Zinnias are sun lovers, and while they tolerate almost any soil, reach perfection in a rich garden loam that is watered deeply in dry weather. In humid weather, they suffer from mildew and so need spraying or dusting with a fungicide early in the growing season and thereafter every ten days. Plants come into bloom quickly and if faded flowers are promptly removed they will bloom until frost. There are so many sizes, heights, and forms that an entire garden could be filled with zinnias. Colors are rich and varied from pinks to reds, yellow to orange, fuchsia and purple, white and yellow, even a green called 'Envy'. There are cactus and dahlia-flowered giants with 6-inch blooms, dwarfs with double blooms only an inch across, and intermediates with 2- to 4-inch blooms. Zinnias are fine for beds and borders, to fill gaps in shrubbery, to overplant bulbs, and for temporary hedges. Recommended tall zinnias include the Zenith strain, Burpeana Giants, and the Dahlia- and Cactus-flowered Hybrids; among intermediates, Fantasy and Zipasee strains; of the miniatures or dwarfs, 'Cupid', 'Daisy Mae', 'Mini-Pink', 'Sugar 'n Spice', and 'Tom Thumb'. Walter Haring photo

Crabapple walk in the author's garden. Walter Haring photo.

PINK TO ROSE

PINK gives to the garden a delicate, at times ethereal, quality that cannot be supplied by any other pastel color. Some pale pinks are more like a touch or emanation than a dye, and we marvel that any flower can be so exquisite. Is there a greater enchantment than the pink clouds of flowering peaches, plums, cherries, and crabapples in spring or the luscious tones of roses and peonies in June?

Rose shades are the delightful transition between light pinks and the carmine and crimson reds. They fulfill the color gap and combine beautifully with white and blues, but are not compatible with all colors, notably rich yellow and orange. There are also the occasional high-keyed even strident pinks and the magentas, which must be very carefully placed. Use the true pinks lavishly as a mass effect or as most accommodating companion plants.

ABELIA *grandiflora*
bush-arbutus   3 to 6 feet

SHRUB. This has been called the perfect shrub, combining graceful habit, small shiny leaves, abundant bloom from June to October, and adaptability to various soils, although a soil enriched with organic matter and a location in sun or semishade are preferred. Not too hardy in the North, it does flourish in many Connecticut gardens and in protected gardens elsewhere in New England and New York. If winter-damaged, it will send up new shoots in spring. Flowers are bell-shaped in a delicate shade of pink. For foundation planting, abelia is excellent, also in groups of rhododendron, azalea, and andromeda. The bronze winter foliage makes a fine contrast to the darker green of evergreens. A. B. Morse Company photo

ACHILLEA *millefolium*
rosy milfoil   2 to 3 feet

PERENNIAL. This is a fine plant for the midsummer garden, with soft ferny foliage, staunch stems, and flat deep pink or white flowers. Even in poor dry soil, it flourishes and spreads rapidly. You can easily separate the clumps in fall, or raise new plants from spring-sown seed. No insects or diseases bother it. Cut arrangements are unusual and keep well. An interesting planting would be with false-dragonhead, hardy pinks, and baby's-breath. Walter Haring photo

AETHIONEMA *grandiflorum*
Persian stone-cress   8 to 10 inches

PERENNIAL. Many gardeners consider this one of the finest rock-garden plants, needing little care, and forming mats of soft green foliage. In late April or early May the racemes of pink or rose flowers, rather like candytuft, stand up above the leaves. It must have full sun and light dry soil, and the protection of a mulch in normally colder areas. Here 'Warley Rose' makes a splendid plant. The Wayside Gardens Co. photo

ALTHAEA *rosea*
hollyhock   6 to 8 feet

BIENNIAL. This old-time favorite of country gardens is not hardy in colder sections and not reliably hardy anywhere. However, it self-sows so readily that many seedling plants often come through the winter. It should be treated as a biennial. Plants should be set out in spring only, in full sun and rich, moist soil for best results. Seeds, and sometimes plants, are available in many colors or in mixture. Hollyhocks are, of course, fine in groups at the back of the border, or in quantity against fences and walls. Shown here is a group of 'Powderpuffs' hollyhock. The annual varieties, which will bloom in summer from seed sown indoors in March, are usually about 4 feet high. George J. Ball, Inc., photo

AMARANTHUS

Joseph's-coat   3 to 5 feet

ANNUAL. The brilliant and multi-colored foliage of various kinds of amaranthus, like 'Early Splendor' (shown here), is spectacular. The flower clusters are uninteresting and close to the stem, but the leaves are yellow, red, or orange, often of combined colors. Amaranthus is stunning in beds and as accent plants in a mixed border. Full sun brings out the colors, but plenty of water is needed by these plants in dry weather. The varieties 'Aurora', 'Joseph's-coat Improved', and A. *salicifolius* all have foliage of differing shapes and colors. A. *caudatus* has drooping dark-red blossoms or all green, as in the variety 'Green Tassel'. Walter Haring photo

ANEMONE
windflower   6 to 12 inches

TUBER. Of the brilliant-flowered tuberous anemones one species, *A. blanda,* will grow in northern gardens if in a sheltered location and deeply mulched over winter. The starry flowers of deep blue or violet-blue make a sheet of color when plants are well grown. They blend with scillas, arabis, and pansies. Variety *rosea* has flowers of deep rose. Plant the tubers in early fall. If they appear dry when purchased, soak for 24 to 48 hours before planting. *A. coronaria,* the showy florist's flower of late winter, is less hardy, and in the extreme North is better planted in spring for summer bloom. It has large poppylike flowers in rich tones of lavender, violet, red, and in white, above crinkled leaves. The St. Brigid (right) and De Caen strains belong here and are glowingly colorful, worth any effort. W. Atlee Burpee Co. photo

A. *japonica*
windflower   2 to 3 feet

PERENNIAL. The fall-blooming anemone (left) is a most satisfactory and beautiful plant, with large crowns of foliage and elegant flowers on long stems. White, red, rose, or pink petals surround a wreath of golden stamens and green pistil. Unfortunately it is not always hardy in really cold sections but does well in some northern gardens. Rich soil, sun, and abundant moisture are its needs. Blue or lavender Michaelmas daisies and colchicum create enchanting effects with this anemone. The Wayside Gardens Co. photo

ARMERIA *maritima*
thrift, sea-pink   10 to 12 inches

PERENNIAL. This very hardy plant has tufts of grassy foliage and 1-inch globular heads of pink flowers in May and June.

It wants a light soil and sunny situation. It provides considerable color in beds and borders and is often charming in rock gardens. Iris, polemonium, and violas are gay and bright with armeria. The Wayside Gardens Co. photo

AZALEA
(*Rhododendron*)   1 to 5 feet

SHRUB. Botanically, azaleas are a group of rhododendrons having funnelform instead of bell-shaped flowers and a minor difference of flower structure. They need exactly the same soil and cultivation. Generally of lower stature and smaller leaved, azaleas relieve the monotony of too solid plantings of rhododendron. They bloom variously from early spring until late May. Named sorts are available in brilliant or delicate shades of pink, red, lavender, orange, and yellow, and can be selected to fit any color scheme. Of the evergreen azaleas the magnificent "Indian" types are hardy only in the South, the Kurume Hybrids at Philadelphia, and the Gable and Glendale Hybrids farther north except in the coldest areas.

Deciduous azaleas are more satisfactory in the whole tier of northern states. One of the finest deciduous species is *A. schlip-*
penbachi, with clear pink fragrant flowers and leaves turning orange and red in fall. Our native pinkster-flower, *A. nudiflorum*, with pale pink flowers, in May and the white swamp-honeysuckle, *A. viscosum*, white or pink, and fragrant, in June and early July make· good garden plants. The Ghent and Mollis Hybrids—pink, salmon, apricot, terra cotta, soft yellow, and white, are fine in the middle states but indifferently hardy in New England, where they have been supplanted by the Exbury and Knaphill strains. Plant azaleas in moist acid soil in light open shade with protection from wind. Prepare the soil with quantities of peatmoss, leafmold, or well-rotted sawdust. Maintain a deep mulch of redwood, fir bark, or oak leaves over the roots. Fertilize in spring with cottonseed meal or Hollytone. Prune azaleas after flowering but only enough to keep the plants compact. Garden of W. B. Scofield. Walter Haring photo

BEGONIA *semperflorens*
   wax begonia   6 to 12 inches

ANNUAL. Few other plants will produce so much and such continuous bloom from early summer to frost. Leaves are shiny, green or red; waxy flowers in shades of pink, rose, red, and white literally cover the plants. They can make beds of solid color and attractive foregrounds in the border. Set out purchased plants in May in sun or semishade in good soil. Keep them well watered in dry spells. Here 'Linda' looks lovely with salvia 'Royal Purple'. Ageratum, sweet-alyssum, lobelia, dwarf celosia, and dwarf marigolds are a few of many other effective companion plants.

B. *tuberhybrida*
     tuberous-rooted begonia   1½ to 2 feet

TUBER.   This is not a single species but
a group of varied hybrids. The flowers are
single, or double, resembling the rose, car-
nation, or camellia, and from 2½ to 5
inches across in subtle or full tones of many
colors. Start tubers indoors in March; plant
out in May in rich, moist soil where they
will receive 3 to 4 hours of morning sun.
They thrive on the north or east side of
the house but not in deep shade. Keep
them plentifully watered in dry weather.
Tuberous-rooted begonias are not for areas
where summers are very hot, very dry, or
very humid. Lift tubers after frost and store
in plastic bags over winter in a cool place.
These plants are beautiful with ferns.

Facing page: 'Linda', George J. Ball, Inc.,
photo. This page: a rose-form type (above
right), a ruffled camellia-form type (below), and a picotee (below right), Walter
Haring photos

CALLUNA *vulgaris*
 heather   12 to 15 inches

SHRUB. For slopes and rockeries, in front
of shrubs and evergreens or for ground-
covers, this is a fine choice. The evergreen
needle foliage is grayish, the plants covered with rosy-pink or lilac-pink flowers in
late winter. Varieties occur with crimson
or white flowers. Plant in a sunny, airy
place, the soil heavily mixed with peatmoss
and leafmold. Protect tops in winter with
evergreen boughs. Every spring work in
more peatmoss to keep the soil acid. Shear
in very early spring to develop compact
plants. The Wayside Gardens Co. photo

CAMELLIA *japonica*   5 to 20 feet

SHRUB. This celebrated Oriental beauty
is reliably hardy only south of Washington, D.C., and in the Pacific Northwest.
A few plants have been grown in protected
gardens north of New York City. The foliage is shiny and evergreen, the flowers
3 to 5 inches across in shades of pink,
red, white, rose, and variegated. Camellias
bloom from late fall to spring according
to the latitude in which they are grown.
Plant them in deep rich acid soil contain-
ing plenty of peatmoss and top-dress with
manure and peat. The situation should be
semishaded; in their native Japan they
grow wild in forests. *Camellia sasanqua*
(illustrated) is lower-growing, and bushier,
with smaller leaves and smaller but beautifully formed flowers. The Wayside Gardens Co. photo

CANNA   1½ to 5 feet

TUBER. Cannas have strikingly bold, tropical-looking foliage and brilliant large-petaled flowers in shades of red, pink, yellow, and white, from late July until frost. Traditionally used for bedding, they can also be excellent accents in the mixed border. Plant the tubers indoors in March in pots and place the young plants out-of-doors by mid-May. They need rich soil and sun and plenty of water in dry periods. The tubers must be dug and stored like dahlias. This is 'Rosenkavalier'. The Wayside Gardens Co. photo

CERCIS *canadensis*
redbud, Judas-tree   6 to 20 feet

SHRUB OR SMALL TREE. This adds unusual charm to the garden in late April or early May. Before the heart-shaped leaves unfurl, clusters of purplish pink pea flowers spring from every branch and main trunk. It is native to the eastern United States, most often found near ponds in low woodlands. This variety, 'Pink Charm', blooms later, with deep rose flowers. Redbud is lovely behind early yellow tulips and daffodils, or along the edges of woodland walks. It will grow in sun as well as in semishade. The Wayside Gardens Co. photo

CHRYSANTHEMUM *coccineum*
pyrethrum, painted daisy 15 to 30 inches

PERENNIAL. This very hardy perennial with elegant, fine-cut foliage is covered with pink, rose, or white single or semi-double daisies in May and early June. This one is called 'Helen'. It succeeds in rich soil and sun but cannot survive in heavy soil. Divide plants every third or fourth year, and cut them down after June to promote a second flowering in autumn. In dry weather a mulch is beneficial. Columbine, iris, campanula, and blue flax are good complements of color and form. A. B. Morse Company photo

CLEMATIS *lawsoniana* 2 to 8 feet

VINE. The general cultivation of clematis is given on page 122. The lawsoniana hybrids include several spectacular large-flowered varieties in shades of lavender, pink, deep rose, and red, as well as white. They bloom in early summer, or some varieties in August, on old wood. They should therefore be pruned only lightly and infrequently. Among the finest and strongest growing is the magenta-rose 'Ernest Markham'. Walter Haring photo

CLEOME *spinosa*
   spider-flower   2 to 5 feet

ANNUAL. One of the few annuals which grow well all over the United States, cleome is a favorite of many gardeners. Once planted, it will appear year after year from self-sown seed. The plants are tall and the airy flowers are borne on top of long stems. When the flowers drop they are followed by odd and effective seed capsules. The variety shown here is 'Pink Queen'. Cleome can be well used in the background of the border. It combines with pastel zinnias, with cosmos and snapdragons. Plant seed directly in the garden in May in full sun. Any reasonably good soil will suffice. George J. Ball, Inc., photo

CLETHRA *alnifolia*
sweet pepperbush   3 to 6 feet

SHRUB. Our native sweet pepperbush is valued for its spikes of deliciously fragrant flowers in late July and August. The white-flowered form is most often seen. The pink-flowering variety *rosea* is equally beautiful. Plant clethra in sun or semishade in rich soil plentifully supplied with moisture during the summer. It is a very good choice for poolside planting or along small streams and in the wild garden. The Wayside Gardens Co. photo

COLCHICUM *autumnale*
meadow-saffron   10 to 12 inches

BULB. Colchicum resembles a large crocus in shades of lavender, lilac, or rose. In September the leafless flowers appear almost suddenly, close to the ground. There is no sign of leaves until the following spring, and then they are large and must be allowed to yellow and ripen to feed the bulb. A situation where the soil gets rather dry in summer is what they like best, so long as there is ample moisture in spring and fall. Bulbs are available in August and will bloom, even without soil, in three weeks. Because they are leafless when in flower, a surrounding low ground-cover is desirable, but the huge leaves in spring are a factor to remember when deciding where to plant colchicums. Probably the best places are in front of evergreen shrubs or at the edge of woodland. P. deJager & Sons, Inc., photo

COSMOS *bipinnatus*
cosmos   2½ to 6 feet

ANNUAL. For its quantities of pink, rose, dark red, or white flowers in late summer and its lacy light green foliage, cosmos has been a standby of gardeners for generations. New varieties come into bloom in July and continue until frost. Most frequently planted for a quick background, cosmos introduces an oft-needed airiness to perennial borders. For this purpose the medium-height strains are best. Radiance and Sensation Hybrids have very large and very early flowers. 'Sensation' in various colors is shown here. 'Sunset' and 'Fiesta' have bright orange flowers from July to September. Plant the seed directly in the garden in May, in sandy or friable soil. Stake the tall sorts. When transplanting seedlings or purchased plants, set them deeper than they were growing in the flat. Bodger Seeds, Ltd., photo

CRATAEGUS
hawthorn   10 to 20 feet

TREE. No trees are hardier or more easily grown than the hawthorns. This one is *C. maskei*. They are fine as accents and backgrounds in large gardens and will endure city air. They bloom in late April or early May, the twiggy growth covered with clusters of double flowers in white, pink, rose, or scarlet. The autumn fruits are brilliant red in most kinds; best known is 'Paul's Scarlet'. The English May-tree, *C. oxyacantha*, with fragrant white or pink flowers, is quite hardy in New England. Hawthorns will grow on most soils, preferring a good loam with some lime, and enjoy plenty of air and sun. The Wayside Gardens Co. photo

CYCLAMEN   4 to 6 inches

TUBER. Though the familiar florist's cyclamen is not winter hardy except in relatively frost-free areas, two other and equally charming species are reliably hardy north of Washington, D. C. Being in nature plants of open rocky woodlands and hillsides, they are most suitable for the rock garden or semishaded spots under trees. The flowers are smaller than those of the hothouse plant. *Cyclamen europaeum*, from Switzerland and the Balkans, has crimson or deep rose flowers, as fragrant as violets, in August and September. *C. neapolitanum,* the baby cyclamen, of Corsica and South Europe (shown here), has more pointed leaves and soft pink or pure white flowers from September to October, and is faintly scented. The leaves do not appear until a little before the flowers. Both need a generous mixture of leafmold in the soil, some lime, and through the winter a 3-to-4-inch mulch to protect the crowns. Drainage is important. Plants must not dry out or have any standing water. Set out the tubers in spring, those of *C. europaeum* just barely covered, those of *C. neapolitanum* somewhat deeper, as it roots from the upper surface only. Taloumis photo

DAPHNE *cneorum*
garland-flower   1 foot

SHRUB. Generally considered difficult and uncertain, this small evergreen is nevertheless so beautiful that many gardeners keep on growing it until they find just the right soil and place where it succeeds. In early spring and again in autumn, clusters of deliciously fragrant pink flowers terminate every twig. Dwarf size and trailing branches make it ideal for rockeries, stony slopes, and the front of groups of evergreens. It is quite hardy with protection. Give it a sheltered location in sun or semishade and mulch with straw or salt hay during the coldest part of the winter. It seems to thrive in various soils so long as drainage is assured. A. B. Morse Company photo

64

DIANTHUS
garden pinks   6 to 12 inches

PERENNIAL. Hardy pinks have grassy blue-green leaves and clove-scented flowers in shades of pink, red, and white. Some varieties bloom in spring, others in June, and still others all summer if faded flowers are promptly removed. The double ones, as this Double Spring Beauty strain, look like small carnations. *D. plumarius* grows to 12 or more inches and is a riot of very fragrant pink or rose flowers in May and June. *D. deltoides,* the Maiden Pink, has creeping foliage and pink or red flowers in May and June, sometimes throughout the summer. *D. caesius,* the Cheddar Pink, grows to 6 inches with light pink flowers. The last two are mat-forming and delightful in the rock garden. *D. allwoodi* grows to 12 inches with large flowers from white to pink to red, often frilled or deeply cut. 'Gaiety' resembles the old-fashioned laced pinks, its large blush-pink to red flowers overlaid or edged with white or deep colors. It is hardy and blooms all summer. Plant all dianthus in well-limed soil and in full sun. Work in more lime or wood ashes in spring.

D. *chinensis*
annual pinks   10 to 15 inches

ANNUAL. These are more slender and branching than the perennial ones. They flower abundantly in many shades and combinations of pink, rose, and red. 'Baby Doll' is the mixture shown here. Seed sown directly in the garden in May in rich, well-limed soil and in full sun will produce flowers from late June to frost. George J. Ball, Inc., photos

DICENTRA
bleeding-hearts   1 to 2½ feet

PERENNIAL. The hardy, old-fashioned flower *D. spectabilis* (illustrated) has handsome, cut-leaved, blue-green foliage and arching sprays of flowers like little pink or deep rose lockets. It blooms in spring with tulips and forget-me-nots, and is a good border plant. The foliage dies down after blooming, so the place must be well marked to avoid damage by cultivation. *D. eximia* has soft, much divided foliage, loose panicles of rose or pink flowers from May until frost, and seems more appropriate in wilder parts of the garden or in the foreground of shrubs. Plant both species where they are to remain for years, in rich, moist soil in sun or semishade. A. B. Morse Company photo

DIGITALIS *purpurea*
foxglove   3 feet

BIENNIAL. These are stately plants making crowns of large, fuzzy leaves. The flowers are 2 to 3 inches long, rose, white, lavender, or cream, often with spotted throats, as in this mixture. *D. ambigua* has pale yellow flowers and is perennial in protected situations. Plant both species in rich, moist soil in sun or semishade. The biennial ones must, of course, be grown from spring-sown seed to bloom the second summer. Foxglove self-sows readily but resents transplanting. In time of drought plants must be well watered, but they cannot tolerate winter wet. In winter don't cover the crowns with mulch but rather tuck it under the leaves to prevent heaving. Clumps of foxglove are superb with delphinium, lilies, lupines, and heuchera. George W. Park Seed Co., Inc., photo

DIMORPHOTHECA hybrids
star-of-the-veldt, African daisy
1 to 1½ feet

ANNUAL. Attractive light green foliage forms large mounds which are completely covered with bloom from July on. The daisy flowers are crisp and cleancut. White is the typical form, but varieties are available in many shades of yellow, orange, pink, and deeper colors. In the North sow seed in May in the garden. In areas of relatively mild winters seed is sown considerably later for late-winter bloom. Any good garden soil and full sun are all that is needed. A. B. Morse Company photo

ERICA
heath   ½ to 2 feet

SHRUB. These delightful little shrubs with tiny gray-green, overlapping leaves and small pink or rose flowers usually start to bloom in late winter and continue to May. The low-growing ones are beautiful in rock gardens or edging beds and borders if the soil is acid. They must have a fibrous, peaty soil and a sheltered spot in the sun. Protect new clumps with straw or salt hay in winter. Trim the tips immediately after flowering to promote compactness. E. carnea (illustrated), the best known, produces rose-red flowers from February to April. E. vagans has pinkish flowers in summer, E. cinerea, purplish flowers. These three are the hardiest species, the last now naturalized on Nantucket and Cape Cod. A. B. Morse Company photo

ERIGERON *karvinskianus*
fleabane   2 to 2½ feet

PERENNIAL. These daisies have relatively short rays and wide disks. They bloom on rather coarse fuzzy foliage in June and throughout the summer if faded flowers are clipped off. The names of these excellent varieties—'Azure Beauty', 'Pink Jewel', and 'Quaker Lady'—suggest the color range, which extends to deep violet and white. Plants need only average soil and sun for most of the day. Veronica, campanula, Shasta daisy, and other summer flowers go nicely with fleabane. The Wayside Gardens Co. photo

GERANIUM
cranesbill   1 to 1½ feet

PERENNIAL. Hardy geraniums (not to be confused with pelargoniums, commonly called geraniums) have much the same form of leaf and flower as the beautiful wild geranium of our northeastern states. The spreading mounds of foliage renew themselves in summer. Through July and August plants produce a wealth of salver-shaped flowers: violet in *G. ibericum* (shown here) and purplish rose in *G. sanguineum*. Other geraniums are white or pink. They need little attention and provide color that blends softly with other flowers. Plant in sun or shade in rich soil and protect from drying winds. They are easy to raise from seed. The Wayside Gardens Co. photo

GERBERIA *jamesoni*
Transvaal daisy   1½ feet

PERENNIAL. This gorgeous exotic in pink, rose, red, creamy yellow, or orange is best known in the North as a florist's flower. Sharp-pointed daisies 3 to 5 inches across open wide on long stems from a rosette of hairy leaves. Though reliably hardy only as far north as Virginia, gerberia does survive under a deep mulch in some protected gardens of colder zones. It is more safely grown as an annual from seed sown indoors in February. Set out young plants in deep rich soil in sun. Lucky southerners enjoy it all winter as a bedding plant. If a daisy can be an aristocrat, this is it. George J. Ball, Inc., photo

GLADIOLUS   1½ to 5 feet

CORM. A great number of varieties have superb large flowers in almost every imaginable shade of color except pure blue. Some have petals ruffled or frilled. They can be grown in rows for cut flowers, or along a fence, or in groups in the border. For a long season of bloom, plant the corms at two-week intervals from late April to June, 4 to 6 inches deep, 6 to 8 inches apart. If in rows, the rows should be 18 inches apart. To flower well, gladiolus must have full sun. Humus or peatmoss and well-rotted manure should be very well mixed with the soil; the addition of a fertilizer 5-10-5 at the rate of 3 to 5 pounds for each 100 square feet is recommended. Keep well watered. When plants have finished blooming, let the foliage mature for 30 to 40 days; dig the corms to store for the winter. Shake off the soil, cut the foliage down to 3 or 4 inches, dry the corms in the sun for a day or two, then place them flat on trays in a dry place for a month. After they are cured, cut off all the old stems and rub the corms clean. Store them in paper bags at 50 degrees through winter. A. B. Morse Company photo

69

GODETIA *grandiflora*
satin-flower   12 to 15 inches

ANNUAL. Sometimes called "Farewell to Spring," the horticultural forms of this native Californian are in bloom from July until frost. They are fine annuals for far northern or mountainous areas where summers are cool. Low mounds of attractive foliage are covered all over with satiny four-petaled flowers rather like evening primroses but in shades of pink, rose, carmine to lavender, and white. Many have white centers or blotches of deeper color. There are double forms. The variety 'Little Gem' is not over 10 inches high. Start the seed indoors in March or outdoors in May, or do both for a succession of bloom. They like a soil not too rich and a situation in sun or half-shade. In dry weather water copiously and mulch with a little compost. George W. Park Seed Co., Inc., photo

HESPERIS *matronalis*
sweet-rocket   3 feet

PERENNIAL. Along woodland walks or in clumps in the mid-border, this is a handsome and highly fragrant plant. Strong stems put forth long panicles of light or dark pink, white or lavender to purple flowers from early June to August. Not reliably hardy in the North, it self-sows readily and thus perpetuates itself and spreads, particularly in rich moist soil. One sometimes sees great masses of it overgrown in abandoned gardens, for it was a favorite of past generations. George W. Park Seed Co., Inc., photo

70

HIBISCUS *syriacus*
rose-of-Sharon 8 to 10 feet

SHRUB. Nurserymen often call this hardy shrub althaea though that name belongs to the hollyhock, a related plant. The salver-shaped flowers are 3 to 4 inches across, ranging from blue and purple to pink, scarlet, and white, often changing as they age. Hibiscus 'Hamabo', shown here, is a fine deep-toned variety. Plants do not bloom until mid-July or August, when flowering shrubs are few. Hence, this plant is invaluable then. In well-drained soil and sun, rose-of-Sharon grows rapidly into a large bush. The Wayside Gardens Co. photo

IBERIS *umbellata*
globe candytuft 10 to 15 inches

ANNUAL. The annual candytuft produces flowers in rounded clusters, white, pink, rose, or lavender. Seed sown in May where it is to grow will furnish blossoms for about six weeks in midsummer. For continuous bloom sow again in June and July. It is attractive with marigolds, snapdragons, and most other summer flowers. Bodger Seeds, Ltd., photo

KALMIA *latifolia*
mountain-laurel   2 to 6 feet

SHRUB. An outstanding American plant, this broad-leaved evergreen is hardy to New England. The flowers are white to pink, in showy clusters, in June and early July. It belongs in the heath family with rhododendron, azalea, andromeda, and leucothoe, and needs the same acid soil and deep mulch of oak leaves. It is ideal as undergrowth at the edge of woodland. It is often interplanted most harmoniously with azaleas and rhododendrons. Winter sun and wind will burn foliage in exposed situations but new growth comes readily in the spring. Isabel Zucker photo

KOLKWITZIA *amabilis*
beauty-bush   6 to 8 feet

SHRUB. Absolutely hardy even in Vermont, the beauty-bush is well named. In June the arching branches and every twig are covered with small, pale pink bell-shaped flowers, the throats tinged yellow, overwhelming the 3-inch leaves. Hence it makes a spectacular specimen. It is also attractive in the mixed hedgerow or for color at the corner of the house, and is particularly lovely near a blue spruce. The bristly fruits, crowned by the spidery calyx, give the shrub a soft and cloudy look in late summer. Plant in full sun where the soil is well drained, as the beauty-bush dislikes standing moisture at the roots. It takes two to three years to become established, after which it will be covered with profuse bloom every year. A. B. Morse Company photo

LAGERSTROEMIA *indica*
crape-myrtle   10 to 20 feet

SHRUB. Though this is not usually hardy north of Baltimore, specimens have been grown in lower New York State and near the coast in New England in protected locations. It is a large treelike shrub which displays great panicles of pink, white, or purplish flowers for many weeks in summer. In the South we see crape-myrtle frequently as lawn specimens and as hedges. It tolerates hot dry weather, but should have good soil and full sun. The Wayside Gardens Co. photo

LATHYRUS *odoratus*
sweet pea   2 to 6 feet

ANNUAL VINE. Though so well known and liked, sweet peas are not easy to grow. Most of them need a cool moist climate and an open trellis or chicken wire to climb on. The soil should be deeply dug, light and loamy, but not sandy, with liberal enrichment. In the North, sow the seed outdoors in full sun in earliest spring, even late March or, preferably, indoors in individual peat pots to be set out later. In the Upper South, sow in the fall for early spring bloom. In the garden, keep well watered. Cut the flowers daily to promote continuing bloom. A most important aid is a 2-inch mulch of rotted manure to keep the roots cool. Fascinating strains, like this Multiflora mixed, are available today—double, ruffled, streaked, and striped, also low-growing bush types, and some that are even resistant to hot weather. The color range is from palest salmon to crimson and dark maroon, from light blue to violet. A mass effect of one or two colors is delightful behind other midsummer flowers; and yet a mixture of all colors of sweet peas is always harmonious, in the garden or in bouquets. Bodger Seeds, Ltd., photo

LILIUM 'Pink Glory'   2½ to 3 feet

BULB. This handsome lily was derived from crossing *L. auratum* with *L. speciosum* and *L. japonicum*. The last-named parent is one of the most exquisite of all lilies but tender in our climate. The new hybrid has the hardiness of its two other forebears. The flower is carried well away from the stem on a wiry pedicel held out horizontally. The segments of the flower are salmon pink, varying in tone, and each has a pale green mark, forming a little star deep inside the flower. 'Pink Glory' blooms in July and August. Oregon Bulb Farms, Herman V. Wall photo

LUPINUS *polyphyllus*
lupine   2 to 3 feet

PERENNIAL. Vigorous long spikes of pea
flowers ascend from most attractive foliage
in June. These plants are an outstanding
note in a mixed border. The flower spikes
must be cut back when they fade but the
foliage remains attractive all summer. The
colors range from blue to lavender, cream
to white, pink to rose. Lupines like a cool
climate and deep, rich moist soil. They do
not transplant well and dislike lime. Small
plants set in their permanent places each
spring give best results, and these are easily
grown from seed sown indoors in late winter. Russell lupines are a famous strain of
fine hybrids. The picture shows the rose-
colored 'My Castle' near paler pink pyrethrum and 'Silver King' artemisia. Walter
Haring photo

LYTHRUM
loosestrife   3 to 6 feet

PERENNIAL. This extremely hardy plant
was formerly avoided by most gardeners
because of its magenta flowers· and rank
growth. Recently hybridists have created
several varieties of other colors and lower
stature which are very handsome. 'Morden's Gleam' is carmine, 'Morden's Pink' is
a clear shade of pink, and 'Happy' is rose-
red. Small, fluffy flowers are produced on
long spikes from July to September and go
excellently with white phlox, 'Connecticut
Yankee' delphiniums, and Shasta daisies.
Lythrum needs rich soil and much moisture in full sun. Walter Haring photo

MAGNOLIA   6 to 20 feet

TREE. The magnificent magnolias are the earliest of flowering trees in many sections of the country. *M. soulangeana*, the saucer magnolia (above), grows fairly rapidly to 20 feet or more and blooms when quite young. The 6-inch saucers are white or pale pink to purple. *M. stellata*, the star magnolia (right), is of lower stature, with flowers composed of many strap-shaped petals, white or pink. Late frosts may brown its flowers, so a protected situation is advisable. The sweet-bay, *M. grandiflora*, a superb evergreen with fragrant white blossoms in summer is found as far north as Washington, D. C., occasionally farther. Magnolias are difficult to transplant. Purchase only balled-and-burlapped specimens and plant them in spring in warm, rich soil. Don't disturb the earth under magnolias; their feeding roots are close to the surface. Saucer magnolia, A. B. Morse Company photo; star magnolia, The Wayside Gardens Co. photo

MALUS

flowering crabapple   10 to 30 feet

TREE. No other small tree is so spectacular in spring as most varieties of flowering crab, not even the cherries. Crabapples are hardier than cherries and in autumn are hung with fruits like burnished jewels. Some forms are spreading, others upright. Foliage can be purplish or bronzy green like that of *M. floribunda atrosanguinea,* 'Hopa' (illustrated), or 'Redvein', all of which have deep rose-red flowers. 'Dorothea' has double pink flowers in early May and pinkish-red fruit. 'Katherine' is probably the finest white-flowered crab. *M. ioensis plena,* known as Bechtel's Crab, bears fragrant double flowers like small roses in May. It does not bear fruit. The flowers of *M. floribunda* are carmine in the bud, opening to pink, and changing to white. 'Guiding Star', another beautiful white-flowered hybrid, blooms in late April and later has yellow fruit. Flowering crabapples give light shade, are splendid as background to the garden, along wide walks, or focal points in large garden scenes. They bloom with daffodils, narcissus, and tulips. In autumn the fruits attract many birds. But don't plant fruiting kinds near terraces or pools because of the dropping of fruit. Plant these marvelous trees in sun and in any good soil. Fertilize in spring with dried cow manure and superphosphate only for the first two years after planting. Too much feeding tends to promote foliage rather than flowers. Walter Haring photo

MIRABILIS *jalapa*
four-o'clock   1 to 2½ feet

ANNUAL. This old-fashioned plant is perennial in the South but grown as an annual in the North. The tuberous roots can be dug, as are dahlia tubers, and stored through winter. It also self-sows freely. The trumpet-shaped flowers—pink, red, coral, lavender, yellow, or white—open late in the day. Sow seed in May in full sun and good soil. The bushy plants make attractive low hedges along walks and driveways. W. Atlee Burpee Co. photo

OCIMUM *basilicum*
sweet basil   2 feet

ANNUAL. The only really decorative basil is this 'Dark Opal'. Reddish-purple foliage and tiny pink flowers on long stalks make it a beautiful summer bedding plant. Sow seed in late spring in full sun and rich soil. Water copiously in time of drought. It is strikingly handsome as an accent plant in the border with *Begonia semperflorens* and sweet-alyssum, or as a background for pink, rose, or white petunias. Leaves may be dried and used to flavor salads and soups. George W. Park Seed Co., Inc., photo

PAEONIA
peony   3 to 5 feet

PERENNIAL. Plants will live for your lifetime or longer, and are hardy everywhere
in the United States except the Lower
South. The herbaceous peonies are hybrids
of *P. albiflora* and other species. Their
foliage is handsome and relatively disease-
free. The single, double, or semidouble
flowers open from late May through June,
along with columbine, iris, anchusa, campanula, veronica, and heuchera. There are
many named varieties, in shades of pink,
rose, red, and white. 'Mrs. Farrand' (above
right) is one of these. The tree peony, *P.
moutan* or *P. suffruticosa*, is a much-
branched shrub bearing huge single or
semidouble flowers, including yellows, early
in May. It survives in old gardens for generations. Let it keep its woody framework,
pruning only in spring to remove any die-
back. Plant peonies in deep rich soil in
September in the North and in late fall
in the Upper South. Cover crowns with
only 2 inches of soil. Fertilize in November with dry manure and bonemeal, in
spring with superphosphate. Prevent botry-
tis blight of flower buds by spraying or
dusting shoots as they emerge and until
buds show color with Ferbam or Bordeaux
mixture. Cut the foliage of herbacious
peonies to the ground after frost and burn
it. Walter Haring photo

red to scarlet. Foliage is fuzzy and gray-
green. For large blooms, in late May and
June, sow seed in late fall in the North.
Flowers continue to come for six weeks
until the event of very hot weather. For
late-summer and early-fall bloom, sow seed
in June; plants come into bloom quickly
and will continue until cut down by heavy
frosts. Set in full sun and rich soil for the
finest blooms. Drainage must be perfect.
Cornflowers, cynoglossum, salpiglossis, and
anchusa give sparkling effects with these
poppies. Walter Haring photo

PAPAVER *rhoeas*
Shirley poppy   1½ to 3 feet

ANNUAL. Excellent for overplanting bulbs,
these poppies grow rapidly and bear their
papery or silky flowers in many colors,
from delicate pink through rose and brick-

PETUNIA *hybrida*   10 to 18 inches

ANNUAL. However familiar, no annual plant is more popular or useful in almost every type of garden. Cultivation is described on page 107. The variety of forms and colors available seems limitless, as new hybrids are created annually. Among the loveliest are some of the simplest, such as the one shown here. Walter Haring photo

PHLOX *decussata*
   tall phlox   1½ to 4 feet

PERENNIAL. No hardy plant fills the mid-summer border with such masses of color as tall-growing phlox. Its flowers are carried in large trusses of pink to rose, to vivid scarlet, lavender, purple, and white. A rich but not heavy soil in full sun is desirable, and copious water in dry weather. To get the largest flower-heads, reduce each clump to eight stems in late spring. Divide clumps every third or fourth year, retaining younger outside shoots and discarding woody centers. Dust with sulphur if mildew is a problem and to discourage spider mites. Keep faded flower-heads cut to prevent plants from self-seeding. *Phlox decussata* (right) is a group of hybrids and its seedlings may revert to less distinctive parents. Many varieties are available, early blooming, midseason, and late. Phlox is one of the few perennials that can be moved in full bloom; therefore it is wise to purchase them in bloom to be sure of getting the exact shade and color you desire. The Symons-Jeune varieties have very large panicles and are most hardy and reliable. Walter Haring photo

80

P. *drummondi*
   annual phlox   6 to 18 inches

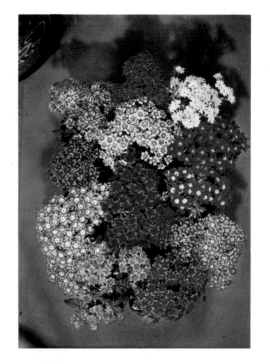

ANNUAL. This pretty plant is very easy to grow. From late June to frost it produces showy clusters of pink, soft yellow, rose, lavender, or red flowers. Plant in rich but light soil and in full sun. Seed sown directly in the garden in early May will develop plants that start to bloom in July. There are varieties for every use: tall ones such as 'Giant Tetra' and 'Glamour' with large flowers, very low-growing types known as *nana compacta,* and intermediates. 'Twinkle' (right) with star-shaped florets is a lovely variety of a distinct type. George J. Ball, Inc., photo

P. *subulata*
   mountain-pink, rock-pink   6 to 8 inches

PERENNIAL. In late April this popular and dependable plant (right) makes sheets of color, and throughout the summer most attractive mats of dense foliage. It is invaluable for covering bare sandy spots and banks as its tangle of fibrous roots binds the soil. This phlox is almost indispensable in the rock garden and excellent as a foreground in the herbaceous border. The soil should be light and not too rich, the clumps lifted and replanted every fourth autumn. The flower colors are pink, rose, blue, lavender, or white. Walter Haring photo

PHYSOSTEGIA
false-dragonhead, obedient plant

2 to 4 feet

PERENNIAL. Very hardy and long-lived, this plant always looks well, the foliage a fresh bright green, the abundant pink, lavender, or white flowers opening on stiff stems. The effect is colorful but cool-looking in July and August. A most rewarding plant, it will grow in any soil and it spreads rapidly. Divide the planting every second year. Almost indispensable in a perennial border, it can also be naturalized in the wild garden. George W. Park Seed Co., Inc., photo

POLYGONUM *orientale*
prince's-feather

3 to 5 feet

ANNUAL. Large, rather coarse leaves, a branching habit, and arching spikes of rose-colored flowers from mid-July to frost make this a fine plant for background or temporary hedge. It will grow in any reasonably good soil in sun or light shade. It transplants without difficulty and self-sows. Attractive combinations are with anchusa 'Blue Bird', blue salvia, *Eupatorium coelestinum,* ageratum, and phlox. Walter Haring photo

PORTULACARIA *grandiflora*

portulaca, rose-moss   6 to 8 inches

ANNUAL. These gay and sparkling little flowers are equally at home in desert areas and where summers are cool. The stems are dwarf and creeping, the foliage needle-like and succulent. The cupped flowers of pink, rose, salmon, orange, scarlet, lavender, or white come into bloom quickly and continue throughout the summer. Portulaca can be planted as late as early July in the North for quick cover of bare places. Full sun is essential; the flowers do not open on gray days. This plant is excellent for dry banks, makes brilliant displays in beds or borders and in sunny spots of the rockery. It self-sows freely. George J. Ball, Inc., photo

PRUNUS
flowering cherry, plum, almond

3 to 20 feet

TREE. This genus includes the ornamental as well as the orchard species of cherries, plums, apricots, peaches, and almonds. They are trees of spectacular spring splendor. Most garden kinds have double flowers of white, pink, rose, or red. Varieties of the so-called Japanese cherry, *P. serrulata,* are often sold today under Oriental names, two of the finest being 'Kwanzan', of erect habit with dangling clusters of rich pink flowers in late April, and 'Shirotae', widespreading, with snow-white bloom. The weeping cherry is *P. subhirtella pendula,* and *autumnalis* is its fall-flowering variety.

Flowering plums are equally beautiful and hardier in very cold sections. *P. pissardi* has white flowers (its variety *rosea* has pink flowers in April); 'Newport' is covered with smaller vivid pink flowers in May—both with purplish-bronze foliage through the summer.

The flowering-almond, *P. triloba* (illustrated), is more like a shrub, with pink or white flowers scattered along every branch in mid-May. The double-flowering almond, *P. glandulosa,* is a low-growing shrub with arching branches covered with fluffy pink flowers, especially good in the foreground of other shrubs. Of these and other kinds of Prunus, no garden should be without a few, as they are the incarnation of spring and will grow with no special care in any loamy, well-drained soil. The Wayside Gardens Co. photo

RHODODENDRON   1½ to 15 feet

SHRUB. Rhododendrons are generally considered the aristocrats of hardy shrubs. Their habit is vigorous and branching, the large leaves evergreen and the flowers wonderfully presented in clusters of pink, rose, lavender, purple, red, or white. Different kinds bloom from May to early July. The American species R. catawbiense, R. maximum, and R. carolinianum are hardy, tall growing, and satisfactory. They have been cross-bred with Asiatic species to create flowers of finer and greatly varied colors. There are so many hybrids that one must consult a specialist's catalogue, but most varieties look well together, except of course, the magentas and reds. 'Scarlet Pimpernel', 'Cadis', 'America', and 'Sky-glow' are a few fine ones. Of the dwarf varieties, 'Blue Tit' and 'Christmas Cheer' are recommended, growing not over 18 inches high. Plant rhododendron in acid soil rich in organic matter, in semishade, or on the north or east side of a building, or where sheltered by evergreen trees. Keep well watered in summer and maintain a deep permanent mulch of peatmoss, fir-bark chips, or oak leaves. Feed in spring with cottonseed meal or a fertilizer made for acid-loving plants. (See also *Azalea*.) The Wayside Gardens Co. photo

ROSA
rose   8 inches to 10 feet

SHRUB. Most roses are surprisingly easy to grow, provided they are properly planted and cared for. The bugaboos of former times—aphids, beetles, leaf-hoppers, black spot, and mildew—can today be quickly controlled by all-purpose sprays or dusts. Diligently looked after, many roses will bloom all summer and well into the fall. The main types of bedding roses are: Hybrid Teas, with one flower on each stem and mostly blooming all summer; Polyanthas, low-growing, with clusters of small flowers, fine for massed beds and edging; Floribundas, a cross between these two—vigorous, tall, greatly varied, the flowers large and in loose branching clusters; and Grandifloras, which are really only a superb form of Floribundas. There are also the old-time Tea Roses, deliciously scented but rather weak and tender except in the South; the exquisite Miniature Roses; the Ramblers, with long, supple, quick-growing shoots and small flowers in dense clusters; and the Climbers, of stiffer, more upright habit and larger flowers, especially the Hybrid Climbers. The Shrub Roses include the centuries-old cabbage rose, musk rose, and moss rose, having scattered, many small-petaled flowers mostly in mid-summer, and the lovely Sweetbrier, with delicate single flowers and foliage of fresh-apple fragrance.

The roses illustrated on this page are 'Rhonda' (above), The Conard-Pyle Company photo, and 'Fairy' (left), The Wayside Gardens Co. photo. On the facing page are shown 'Gene Boerner' (top) and 'Pascali' (center), All American Rose Selections photos, 'Chrysler Imperial' (bottom left), Walter Haring photo, and 'Angel Face' (bottom right), All American Rose Selections photo

There are roses for every kind of garden and situation. Climbers can provide background, cover arbors, and porches. Shrub roses combine well with other low shrubs, one type, *R. rugosa,* making an impenetrable hedge and having brilliant autumn fruits. Trailing roses are for banks and rocky places. Plant all roses in early spring or late fall where they will receive full sun or at least six hours of sun a day, in soil which has been plentifully enriched with bonemeal and peatmoss. Place the bud union just below the surface. Spray or dust weekly throughout the growing season with an all-purpose rose insecticide and fungicide to control pests and disease. Water deeply once a week, letting water from the hose flow gently around each bush. Avoid overhead watering, to minimize the danger of fungus diseases. In early spring and again in July apply rose fertilizer. In November after frost spread dried cow manure and bonemeal over the bed. In cold sections, protect with a cone of soil over the lower ten inches of the plant. If your soil is on the acid side, give lime every three years.

SCABIOSA *atropurpurea*
pincushion-flower   1 to 2 feet

ANNUAL. The rounded compound flower-heads of this plant are stuck all over with white or light-colored anthers like so many pins. The colors run from velvety dark purple through lavender, blue, and pink, as in this 'Coral Moon', and yellow to white. Sow seed in May where it is to grow, a sunny spot of good soil. Since the foliage is rather scant, the proximity of better-foliaged plants makes a better effect. Bodger Seeds, Ltd., photo

SEDUM
stonecrop, live forever   3 to 12 inches

PERENNIAL. Out of the hundreds of species found all over the world only a few are hardy and amenable to our climate. They are mostly succulents, liking dry conditions and poor soil, forming clumps or mats. *S. spectabile* and *S. sieboldi* (illustrated) are the largest, having wide umbels of rose-colored flowers on 12-inch stems in late summer. The foliage is a cool light green and always attractive. *S. acre* and *S. sarmentosum* are creeping, with yellow flowers in late spring. *S. spurium* has pink or crimson flowers on 6-inch stems above shining leaves in summer. All bloom best in full sun and give an interesting change of foliage texture and color. In the rock garden or as ground-cover the creeping sorts can be a menace to other plants if not restrained. The Wayside Gardens Co. photo

88

SIDALCEA *malvaeflora*
checker-bloom   1½ to 2 feet

PERENNIAL. This pretty little plant is valuable for the pink garden or the mixed border, being of easiest cultivation. Cupped flowers, 1½ inches across, are borne hollyhock-fashion on sturdy stems, from July to mid-September. In full sun in any good soil, and with plenty of moisture in time of drought, sidalcea will provide quantities of rose-pink flowers. They are delightful with phlox, Shasta daisy, and Michaelmas daisy. The Wayside Gardens Co. photo

TALINUM *paniculatum*
jewels of Opar   2 feet

ANNUAL. Though seldom seen, this is an interesting and readily grown annual in northern gardens. The foliage is succulent and pale green, to about 10 inches high, unaffected by pests or disease. The tiny pink flowers are borne on long sprays, making a hazy effect. After the flowers drop, small ruby-red beadlike seed-pods appear and hang on until frost. The sprays of seedheads can be cut and dried for winter bouquets. In full sun and in good soil, talinum will flower for weeks in midsummer. Sow the seed indoors in March or out of doors in May. This plant is lovely edging a narrow walk, either alone or with lobelia or ageratum. George W. Park Seed Co., Inc., photo

TAMARIX
tamarisk   6 feet

SHRUB. The light and airy character of this shrub adds a distinct note to any garden. Both the foliage and the long branching panicles of pink flowers have a feathery or fluffy look. It will grow in any good soil a little on the acid side in full sun, and being tolerant of salt air is most useful for seaside gardens. Newly set plants should be cut back to within 8 inches of ground level; and many gardeners recommend keeping the mature plants pruned to 3 or 4 feet. 'Pink Cascade' (illustrated) and 'Summer Glow' are very good varieties, like rosy clouds when in bloom in late summer. The Wayside Gardens Co. photo

THYMUS
decorative thyme   3 to 8 inches

PERENNIAL. Thymes are actually very small shrubs with highly aromatic leaves in off-shades of green. *T. citriodorus,* lemon-scented, has small pink flowers in terminal clusters. Creeping thyme, *T. serpyllum,* has rosy purple flowers, or white or pale pink in some varieties (illustrated), and is invaluable for planting between flagstones or terrace paving. Both bloom in late June, are very hardy, and excellent for the rockery. The tiny evergreen leaves turn bronze in autumn. Plant thyme in full sun and light sandy loam. It will grow in quite shallow earth and in very dry places, and spreads rapidly into dense mats. Walter Haring photo

VALERIANA *officinalis*
hardy garden-heliotrope   3 to 5 feet

PERENNIAL. This valerian is a showy plant in June with very fragrant pinkish flowers in branching umbels over finely cut foliage. Long-lived, it is often found in old gardens, needing only any good soil and a sunny place, but doing best in a soil of high lime content. There are forms with deep pink or white flowers. Cats are very fond of the roots and stalks of this plant and can be quite destructive. A. B. Morse Company photo

WEIGELA   3 to 6 feet

SHRUB. Hardy and deciduous, easy to grow, this shrub blooms in late May and June, covering itself with sprays of showy flowers in shades of pale pink, rose, or garnet. Plant in early spring or late fall in average soil in a sunny location. If the season is very dry, water freely. Prune after flowering, cutting back those shoots that have bloomed to the side branches that have not yet produced flowers, and cut out a few hard old canes at the base. Good varieties include 'Bristol Ruby' and 'Newport Red', with deep-red flowers, the pink-flowered 'Rosea', and the darker rose 'Boskoop Glory'. Walter Haring photo

Dwarf burning-bush in the author's garden. Walter Haring photo.

RED

RED is of course the warmest and strongest color. Eye-compelling, it will be a focal point wherever placed. Exhilarating, exciting, and dramatic effects can be achieved with red flowers. Paradoxically, the stimulus of too much red can quickly pall, like prolonged loud music. Use it with restraint and imagination. Intense and distressing color clashes occur when scarlet or vermilion is adjacent to pale pink or rose. Surround and subdue these spectacular accents with the quieting tones of lavender-blues, whites, and greens. And don't overlook the many possible combinations of brilliant red with gray-leaved or whitish-leaved plants.

Not all reds are flame color. Deep rich velvet reds, garnet, mahogany, port wine, russet, and maroon occur in a surprising number of flowers and can provide delightful tapestry effects with flowers of other colors. Reds are the spices of the garden, but like their culinary counterparts should be used sparingly and occasionally.

BEGONIA *tuberhybrida*
   (hanging-basket type)   1½ to 2 feet

TUBEROUS. Of fairly recent development, this group of begonias is a great addition to the number of plants which will flower well and for a long period in shade. They are available in many tones of pink, rose, red, yellow, and white, and need no special care beyond the usual preparation of lining the basket with moss or sphagnum and watchful watering. For shaded sitting areas or suspended against a north-facing wall they contribute delightful, prolific bloom. The vermilion variety illustrated is planted with maidenhair fern. Brown's Bulb Ranch photo

CELOSIA *argentea*
   cockscomb   1 to 4 feet

ANNUAL. These interesting plants produce very showy branching panicles or spikes or rounded crests of numerous close-set tiny flowers throughout summer to frost. Variety *cristata* has flower-heads resembling the rooster's comb, large, velvety, in rich shades of red, scarlet, rose, purple, yellow, and chartreuse. *C. argentea* 'Forest Fire' (illustrated) has silky plumes on very long stems. Others have various bizarre shapes. Sow seed directly in the garden in May in good soil and sun. For early bloom, sow seed indoors in April. Celosias are prized for dried winter bouquets. Walter Haring photo

CHAENOMELES *japonica*
flowering-quince   2 to 6 feet

SHRUB. The hardy "japonica" of old gardens with its brilliant flowers of orange-red is usually listed in catalogues as *Cydonia* (which is a related plant, the edible quince). In very early spring, japonica is most showy, its thorny stems covered with flowers of blazing hue. Varieties with white, pink, or red flowers, like this one called 'Knaphill Scarlet', are available. The greenish fruits may be used for making jelly. It will thrive for years in any garden soil in sun or semishade. Isabel Zucker photo

COTONEASTER   2 to 4 feet

SHRUB. Of the many cotoneasters the most valuable ones in the garden are various hardy evergreen low-growing species. The shrubby branches are covered with small, dark green leaves, in spring with a foam of tiny pink blooms, and in the fall with bright red berries. Most of them are spreading, perfect for clothing banks or spilling over walls. Plant in sun or half-shade in any good well-drained soil. A. B. Morse Company photo

DIANTHUS *barbatus*
sweet-William   15 inches

BIENNIAL. This has been long cherished for its fragrance and quaint beauty. The dense rounded flower-heads are often 4 inches across composed of 20 to 30 small "pinks" in rich and velvety shades of rose, scarlet, crimson, white, or bicolored. Seed sown in early spring produces good-sized plants that overwinter to bloom in June of the next year. Spring-purchased plants are best treated as annuals. In any good soil and full sun, with reasonable care, they will thrive. Sweet-William is charming in small clumps throughout the perennial border; it provides flowers just at that dull period between early and midseason perennials. Walter Haring photo

EMILIA *sagittata*
tassel-flower   1½ feet

ANNUAL. This attractive plant thrives in full sun and in any good soil. It should be crowded to produce a good show, as the flowers are composed of quite small and bunched florets. From mid-July until frost, they are borne in ¾-inch clusters on long stems, scarlet as in this variety, *coccinea,* or golden yellow to orange in the variety *lutea.* Marigolds go well with them; white petunias or white snapdragons set off their bright color. Or try blue-lace-flower for a surprisingly harmonious effect. George W. Park Seed Co., Inc., photo

EUONYMUS *alatus compactus*
  dwarf flame-bush   4 to 6 feet

SHRUB. This fine and low-growing form
of the well-known burning-bush is becoming very popular for its size, its great hardiness, and autumn color. In late September
the leaves turn rosy scarlet and hang on
for weeks. When they fall, the show goes
on with myriads of red and orange fruits.
The bark is corky with pinkish wings. This
shrub will succeed in any good soil in a
sunny location, in front of taller shrubs or
as a low hedge. With a background of evergreens it is particularly effective, as shown
in the photo on page 92.

E. *radicans vegetus*
  bigleaf winter-creeper   20 to 40 feet

VINE. Often called Japanese evergreen
bittersweet, this shrubby vine of great
beauty and hardiness is used to cover
stone or brick walls, to which it clings by
rootlets along the stems. Red or orange
fruits, resembling bittersweet, make a fine
display in late fall and early winter. It can
be pruned to keep it low and shrubby.
Grow in sun or semishade in any soil
which is not too rich. Photo courtesy of
Stern's Nurseries, Geneva, New York

GAILLARDIA
blanket-flower   1 to 2½ feet

PERENNIAL. There are many varieties of this old-time favorite, as various species have been crossed and re-crossed. The typical plant (illustrated) has rather sparse, hairy leaves and large informal daisy flowers with a double ring of yellow, orange, red, or even magenta, often bicolored. The variety 'Burgundy' is wine-red, sometimes tipped with yellow. Gaillardias bloom from June to September, frequently on into the fall if faded flowers are removed. They are of easiest culture in light, well-drained soil, with full exposure to sun and air. In heavy soil or very hard winters they may die out, but they self-sow readily.

ANNUAL. These are similar to the perennial type but not so tall, and they vary greatly in form, from all-double, ball-shaped flowers, as in the Lollipop series, to singles of dark bronzy red. Shasta daisies or other white flowers are attractive near these brilliant flowers, and many blue flowers such as campanulas harmonize well. A. B. Morse Company photo

GEUM *aurantiacum*
avens   1 to 1½ feet

PERENNIAL. Mostly hybrids from a Chilean and southern European species, these plants are of doubtful hardiness in cold climates. The flowers are single or semi-double on long stems above a crown of hairy leaves. They appear in May and then lightly throughout the summer. Geum needs sun or very light shade, adequate moisture in summer and dryness in winter. It does not do well in exposed locations. A sheltered spot in the rock garden is its safest home, but it can be lovely in a well-drained part of the border. Seed sown indoors in March or in the cold frame in April, though taking fifteen to twenty days to germinate, will produce flowers the same year. Good varieties include the well-known double vermilion 'Mrs. Bradshaw' (illustrated) and the yellow-flowered 'Lady Stratheden'. White phlox, Michaelmas daisies, and hardy ageratum are good companions, so too the blue spires of *Campanula persicifolia*. The Wayside Gardens Co. photo

GLORIOSA *rothschildiana*
gloriosa-lily   2 to 3 feet

TUBER. A climber, this is a fascinating and exotic plant for the summer garden in the North. It clings by tendrils at the leaf tips and requires some kind of support. The late-summer flowers have six waved and reflexed petals of orange and yellow that turn dark red with age. In India they are called tiger's claws. In frost-free areas the odd-shaped tuber may be left in the ground after bloom is finished and the plant dies down. In the North, set each tuber slantwise in a 6-inch pot in February or March and transplant out of doors in mid-May to a place of full sun and rich soil. The tubers are very brittle and must be carefully handled so as not to injure the budding end. In fall they may be lifted and stored as you would cannas. W. Atlee Burpee Co. photo

GOMPHRENA *globosa*
globe-amaranth   2 feet

ANNUAL. The sturdy and pretty little gomphrenas will grow anywhere in the United States reckless of heat and drought. Much-branched plants produce thimbles or globes of deep purple, white, rose, or orange from mid-season to frost. 'Buddy' is illustrated. For early bloom sow indoors in March, for midsummer bloom outdoors in May. They hold their color for dried bouquets. George J. Ball, Inc., photo

HEUCHERA *sanguinea*
  coralbells   1½ to 3 feet

PERENNIAL. One of the finest plants for beds, borders, and rockeries, this is easy to grow and hardy even in cold areas. Small red, as in 'Fire Sprite' (illustrated), or rose or white nodding bells are borne on long racemes over attractive foliage that turns reddish in winter. From June to August in northern gardens, these airy flowers will lighten any planting, and work magic as an edging in a rose garden. Suggested companion plants are feverfew, *Digitalis ambigua*, campanula, veronica, and anthemis. The Wayside Gardens Co. photo

IMPATIENS
busy-Lizzie, sultana   8 to 24 inches

ANNUAL. *I. holsti* and *I. sultani* are much alike, the former taller and more bushy. Widely known as indoor plants, they are good also as bedding annuals in northern gardens and available in shades of pink, rose, red, and in white. The Imp series is illustrated here. They will bloom profusely in light shade provided they are kept well watered in time of drought and generously fed. Start seed indoors in March at 70°F. Don't set plants out until weather and soil conditions are really warm. They revel in warm summers, but not in direct sun or windy locations. Begonias and coleus make interesting combinations with impatiens and like the same situation.

I. *balsamina*
lady-slipper   1 to 2½ feet

ANNUAL. Often listed as balsam, this is an old favorite, sturdy, floriferous, and quaint, with its leafy stalks of double camellia-like flowers in many shades of pink, lavender, and red, as shown below. It is easy to grow in beds and borders. Sow seed in May where plants are to remain, in any good soil and in sun. Edge with ageratum for an attractive all-summer picture. Walter Haring photos

LOBELIA *cardinalis*
  cardinal-flower   3 to 4 feet

PERENNIAL. Found growing at the very edge of streams or in marshy tangles, this fascinating American plant takes readily to cultivation. Its red flowers have an unusual and sharply cut pattern, and they come in midsummer for several weeks, in sun or part shade. They are at their best in a bog garden but will grow well in a border if the soil is rich, on the acid side, moist, and well drained. Striking combinations are possible with white phlox, early white chrysanthemums, and blue lobelia. Walter Haring photo

LYCHNIS *chalcedonica*
  Maltese cross   2 to 4 feet

PERENNIAL. Flowers are fiery red in flat clusters on long rigid stems. The plant is of easiest cultivation in sun in rich, moist soil. The leaves are apt to be thin and inconspicuous, so it is best placed near other plants of good foilage, such as chrysanthemum or cerastium. There are varieties with white or pink flowers. Lychnis blooms in late June and July with the Shasta daisies and daylilies. George W. Park Seed Co., Inc., photo

MONARDA *didyma*
bee-balm, bergamot   3 to 5 feet

PERENNIAL. This used to be called the Fourth-of-July plant because the bright red, raggedy blooms first open in early July. The foliage is most pleasantly aromatic. 'Cambridge Scarlet' (illustrated) is a standard variety. Others have pink, lavender, purplish, dark red, or white flowers. Bold clumps in full sun and in any soil add massed color to the midsummer border, especially fine with Shasta daisy, phlox 'Miss Lingard', and coreopsis. Bee-balm needs plenty of water in dry spells and division of roots every second spring. Walter Haring photo

PAPAVER *orientale*
Oriental poppy   3 feet

PERENNIAL. The cupped flowers are enormous, in tones of yellow, orange, red, white, pink, salmon, rose, and lavender. Bloom occurs in late May and early June with the peonies, painted daisies, columbine, coralbells, and iris. The coarse, fuzzy foliage dies down soon after blooming is over but appears again in early autumn to stay green over winter. Plant in rich soil, in full sun. Give bonemeal in fall and a liberal side-dressing of dried cow manure and superphosphate early in spring. These poppies are best moved in fall but can be moved in spring if a large root ball is taken with each plant. Illustrated are a double-flowered form 'Crimson Pom' and the red-and-white variety 'Carnival'. Walter Haring photos

PELARGONIUM
geranium   10 to 18 inches

ANNUAL. The familiar geraniums are cultivated hybrids of South African species, actually perennials too tender to survive our northern winters out of doors. We treat them as annuals from seed sown indoors in February in warmth—the new Carefree strain (illustrated) blooms in three to four months—or grow them from spring-purchased plants. Set outdoors in mid-May in full or part sun, in good soil, with plenty of moisture in time of drought, they will begin to bloom about the first of July. Some have leaves with zones of deeper green or bronze. The flowers make masses of color—pink, salmon, rose, red, or white —and can provide endlessly interesting effects with petunias, ageratum, sweet-alyssum, lobelia, and many others. Potted geraniums can be dropped into the border to supply immediate color. George J. Ball, Inc., photo

PENSTEMON
beard-tongue   2 to 4 feet

PERENNIAL. There are about 150 species
of this American plant, of which some are
hardy in the North. They have showy
spikes of many trumpet blooms, but otherwise vary from tall plants for the back of
the border to lower ones for the rock garden, and there are even some prostrate
creeping kinds. Colors range from red, as in
this 'Firebird', and pale pink to rose, coral,
purple, blue, and white. The foliage is
light green, sometimes gray-green or bluish,
usually bushy and disease-free. Plants come
into bloom in June and continue over a
long period in summer. *P. grandiflorus*,
with pale lavender flowers, and *P. digitalis*,
white, are two hardy tall species. P. 'Sensation' grows to 2½ feet, with flowers from
pink to crimson. *P. pygmaeus* and *P. hir-
sutus* are beautiful lavender-flowered rock
plants. All penstemons are easily grown
from seed sown in spring. They like a
sunny situation in any good soil and need
adequate moisture through summer. The
Wayside Gardens Co. photo

PETUNIA *hybrida*   1 to 2 feet

ANNUAL. Petunias are among the finest
of annuals for continuous bloom and are
known and loved the country over. 'Red
and White Magic' (right) are a handsome
sight. Flowers keep coming from early summer until hard frost, in every conceivable
tint and shade, including now some almost blue and almost black. Different forms
have been bred for various purposes and
situations: dwarfs for edging and bedding;
balcony and window-box types; cascades
for hanging baskets or to trail down from
rock walls; ruffled, fringed, double-flowered, and giant size for mass display. Each
year hybridizers give us so many gorgeous
new varieties that the descriptions fill pages

in catalogues. Their great range of color, ease of cultivation, and prolific bloom make them adaptable to any color scheme with other flowers. Annuals that will combine with petunias most colorfully are ageratum, celosia, geraniums, lobelia, marigolds, salvia, sweet-alyssum, and zinnias. Florists and garden centers offer well-started plants. For a long season of bloom, seed is best sown early indoors. Being very small, it should not be covered, just lightly pressed into the soil. In late spring, set out young plants in rich garden soil and full sun. In midsummer cut back straggly ends to shape the plant and to keep it producing new flowers. Pot some plants in fall for winter bloom indoors. George J. Ball, Inc., photo

PYRACANTHA *coccinea*
firethorn   6 feet

SHRUB. The branches of this evergreen shrub are indeed thorny and the foaming white spring flowers rather modest, but not so the eye-catching, deep orange autumn berries. There is also an excellent form with yellow berries. Pyracantha lends itself readily to espalier, can be trained against walls, fences, or around doorways, and is also useful as a foundation plant. It needs an open spot in full sun or light shade. Though the foliage may burn in late winter, new leaves soon put forth. To train it against a wall, select enough strong canes, cut the rest away, and attach with vine hooks. Here a yellow-red pyracantha looks handsome against a wall. The Wayside Gardens Co. photo

ROSA
rose   3 to 5 feet

BUSH. Floribunda roses produce their flowers in clusters on long stems. They are hardy, sturdy, and the habit of growth is bushy. 'Firecrest' (shown here) is one of the finest, the crimson flowers of good substance and the foliage deep green. In beds, in front of shrubs, or as a hedge, it is excellent, growing to about 3 feet. The Wayside Gardens Co. photo

R. 'Comanche', 4 to 5 feet, an All American Award Winner, is a Grandiflora, a vigorous type, taller than the Floribundas. The orange-red blooms 3½ to 4 inches across are fully double with some fifty petals; the young leaves have a bronze tint. The Conard-Pyle Company photo

SALVIA *splendens*
scarlet sage   1 to 3 feet

ANNUAL. However familiar and often seen in discordant bedding schemes, this brightest of red-flowered plants can create fascinating effects when thoughtfully used. The foliage is dark green and vigorous. The bracts, the calyx, and the corolla are all scarlet. In flower from August to late fall, it is particularly welcome in the autumn garden. There are dwarf varieties, such as 'Scarlet Pygmy' and 'Flarepath'; medium-heights like 'St. John's Fire' (illustrated) and 'America'; and tall ones to 3 feet that can provide a temporary hedge or background. For early bloom, sow the seed indoors in late February or March and transplant to the garden after any danger of frost. Or obtain young plants from a nursery in May. Gray- or whitish-leaved plants, the dusty millers, and some ornamental grasses are the perfect foil for *Salvia splendens*. Combine it with white petunias and *Salvia farinacea* 'Blue Bedder' or ageratum for a summer-long picture. George J. Ball, Inc., photo

SPREKELIA *formosissima*
Aztec-lily, St.-James-lily   1 to 2 feet

BULB. This tender Mexican bulb is valued for its early-summer bloom. Solitary bright red flowers open on a slender stalk before the narrow 12-inch leaves develop. After danger of frost has passed, plant 3 inches deep in rich soil in a semishaded location. Flowers appear three to four weeks later. The red sprekelia is charming in the company of blue flowers. Brown's Bulb Ranch photo

TIGRIDIA *pavonia*
Mexican shell-flower   2 to 3 feet

BULB. This is a charming and easy-to-grow tender bulb for the garden in July and August. The flowers have a cup-shaped center, usually elaborately spotted or marked, and flaring petals of white, orange, and buff to flame-red. The plants are most effective in groups in the mixed border. They like full sun and a slightly sandy soil and are happy in seaside gardens. When warm weather comes, plant 2 to 3 inches deep and 4 to 6 inches apart. Leave the bulbs in the ground until frost threatens, then lift and store as you would gladiolus. Brown's Bulb Ranch photo

TROPAEOLUM *majus nanum*

nasturtium   1 foot

ANNUAL. These delightfully scented little plants have nostalgic associations for many people, recalling the bright flower beds of our childhood when we liked to bite into the peppery stems. The rounded, light green leaves make a cool setting for myriads of yellow, orange, cherry, scarlet, or tawny flowers. There are straw-colored, salmon, mahogany, and even purple ones, and somehow they all blend beautifully. Fine popular strains are Jewel Mixed (illustrated), double-flowered Golden Gleam, and Fragrant Giants. Edgings or areas of a single color can brilliantly strengthen many effects with other flowers, particularly of course those which also like a rather light soil. Poppies, coreopsis, marigolds, gladiolus are a few. In a rich soil, nasturtiums will produce more leaves than flowers. For sandy places they are a boon. Full sun is essential. They will begin to bloom within a month after sowing and go on until frost. The black aphids that almost invariably find them can be readily controlled by a contact dust or spray. Stecher-Traung-Schmidt Corporation photo

111

'Connecticut Yankee' delphinium, gloriosa daisies, and daylilies in the author's garden. Walter Haring photo.

BLUE TO PURPLE

BLUE is the receding color, creating serene and shadowy effects in the garden. Sharing with white flowers the suggestion of coolness, blue flowers also convey a sense of space or distance. In the warmth of summer, scarlet, gold, orange, and bright pinks predominate. Blue will soften and tone down these overly strong colors.

Among all flowers blue ones exhibit the greatest variation of color tone, from the palest blue-violet to the almost-black purple tulip 'Queen of the Night'. Forget-me-nots, pansies, and campanulas each have a blue of their own, and different varieties are different blues. There are green-blues, sky-blues, Cambridge blue, pure blue (not many flowers are pure blue), cobalt, indigo, and endless tones of lavender-blue to purple. This provides great flexibility for the generous use of this important color in the planting scheme. Scarlet salvia is emphasized by light blue ageratum at its feet. Pale yellow petunias are brilliant with dark blue annual larkspur. And many combinations of blue look well together, as in mixed varieties of iris or delphinium. A planting of light lavender crocus or of tulips will be enhanced by a few bulbs of much deeper lavender here and there.

It is considered very difficult to create a successful garden entirely of blue flowers, though they may well be the center of interest. It is difficult for me to conceive of any garden without some components of this mysterious and refreshing color.

113

AGERATUM *coelestinum*
floss-flower   3 to 12 inches

ANNUAL. The well-known lavender-blue ageratum is one of the most useful and dependable annuals, lavish with fluffy flower-heads from July until frost. 'Blue Mist' is illustrated. It needs only average soil, at least six hours of sun each day, and generous watering in time of drought. Sow seed indoors in February or March or in the coldframe in April, because ageratum takes time to come into bloom. Warmth is necessary for good germination. Or young plants can be found at local nurseries in May. Usually seen as an edging, ageratum can also be fitted into the front of the border, or grown in window boxes, set at the base of a birdbath, or in formal beds, where it seems to look well with other flowers of any color or with mixed colors, even scarlet sage and bright zinnias. It is particularly attractive with marigolds, bedding dahlias, and snapdragons. George J. Ball, Inc., photo

AJUGA *genevensis*
bugle-plant   4 to 5 inches

PERENNIAL. For rockeries, edgings, and ground-covers, this is one of the best plants, spreading fast in sun or shade. Thick rosettes of foliage send up short spikes of lavender-blue flowers in late spring. *A. reptans* is very similar but with smaller spikes in white and pink as well as blue, and in bronze-leaved and dark-red-leaved forms. Although very hardy, it may winter kill if the temperature goes below zero with no snow cover. Primulas and *Iberis sempervirens* bloom at the same time. Late-flowering bulbs such as *Scilla hispanica* and Darwin tulips are well placed with ajuga. A. B. Morse Company photo

ANCHUSA *capensis*
summer forget-me-not   1½ feet

ANNUAL. Although this is biennial in mild climates, it seldom survives severe winters, and north of Virginia is usually grown as an annual. The variety 'Blue Bird' is outstanding; the foliage is green and velvety, the flowers deep blue. Good drainage is essential for it to grow well and to produce quantities of flowers from mid-summer to frost. Seed may be sown indoors in March or in the garden in May where plants are to grow. Suited to the rock garden because of the sure drainage there, anchusa will also accord well with petunias, marigolds, and other annuals in the garden proper. A. B. Morse Company photo

ANEMONE *pulsatilla*
pasque-flower   6 to 10 inches

PERENNIAL. In rockeries and gravelly soil elsewhere, when winter has scarcely gone, the big buds of this plant rise out of the ground, looking like silky-haired cocoons. They expand into large lavender or purple flowers. Then the carrotlike foliage appears, to become emerald green tufts in summer. More bloom follows until the end of April or early May. *Tulipa tarda, Alyssum saxatile,* and white arabis make fine effects with this anemone. A. B. Morse Company photo

115

ASTER
Michaelmas daisy   1½ to 4 feet

PERENNIAL. This is the showiest perennial for late August and September. The 1½-inch flowers vary from pale blue to deep lavender, purple, pink, and white, covering much of the branched plants. Borne profusely, they create masses of subtly blended color. The tall kinds are unsurpassed for a background, the medium-heights supply great mounds of bloom. In full sun and rich loamy soil they do best. Divide the clumps each spring, planting outside shoots and discarding woody centers. Formosum lilies (*lilium longiflorum formosum*) and chrysanthemums may be grown with them for pleasing contrasts. The Wayside Gardens Co. photo

BRACHYCOME *iberidifolia*
Swan-River daisy   14 inches

ANNUAL. With foliage like filigree work and flowers with long rays of blue, lilac, white, or pink, this plant is charming for the edge of beds and borders. From July until mid-August it blooms profusely. Sow seed outdoors in May in a sunny place where plants are to grow. Keep faded flowers cut to prolong the blooming season. W. Atlee Burpee Co. photo

116

BROWALLIA *elata*
amethyst-flower   1 to 1½ feet

ANNUAL. Delightful in beds and in hanging baskets, this plant blooms all summer in sun or part shade in any good soil, but must be started early from seed sown indoors in March. To make a well-branched plant for the garden, the tip and branches of the large variety *grandiflora* need to be pinched out. 'Sapphire' is compact, growing to 12 inches. 'Blue Bells Improved' (illustrated) needs no pinching. Spent flowers should be removed for continuous bloom. George J. Ball, Inc., photo

BRUNNERA *macrophylla*
large-leaved forget-me-not
                    12 to 15 inches

PERENNIAL. Formerly called *Anchusa myosotidiflora* and often still sold under that name, this plant bears great sprays of intense blue flowers in May. In summer the leaves become large and lush and one plant can be divided into many for wide coverage. Plant in rich moist soil in sun or light shade. In the rockery or border it combines well with tulips, late daffodils, the yellow *Alyssum saxatile,* and the hardy white candytuft. Brunnera offers one of the few true blues for the garden. The Wayside Gardens Co. photo

CALLISTEPHUS *chinensis*
China aster   10 inches to 3 feet

ANNUAL. This old favorite among garden flowers has been highly developed in recent years to include scores of named varieties in every shade of every color, and now in notably wilt-resistant strains. There are dwarf, low-growing, and tall kinds, compact cushions, branching, and long-stemmed. The last are unexcelled for cutting. The cactus-flowered type has hundreds of needlelike petals. Any of these supply wonderful color in the late summer garden and suggest endless combinations with other flowers. They like rich soil with plenty of moisture and full sun. Sow seed outdoors in May where plants are to grow or indoors in March for earlier bloom. Walter Haring photo

CAMASSIA *esculenta*
quamash   1½ to 3 feet

BULB. Little-known but hardy and long-lived, this is charming naturalized along woodland walks or grown in small groups in the border. Starry blue-violet flowers in pyramidal racemes rise from coarse grassy foliage. May or June is their season. Plant 5 inches deep in fall where bulbs will not be disturbed. The color varies and is soft and exquisite, best set off by adjacent white or yellow flowers. A. B. Morse Company photo

CAMPANULA *carpatica*
bellflower   4 to 8 inches

PERENNIAL. Of the many species of low-growing campanulas, this is the most reliable and easiest for our gardens, flowering from June to August. Much used in rock gardens, it also makes good clumps in the border foreground. There are blue and violet and white forms, the flower shapes varying from deep cups to wide saucers. 'Cobalt Bell' (illustrated) is a fine variety. Plant in rich soil where the sun shines at least six hours a day. The Wayside Gardens Co. photo

C. *medium*
Canterbury-bells   3 feet

BIENNIAL. These are stately plants for the mid-border, blooming in June and early July. Blue, pink, and white forms are available and look well together. Sow the fine seed in spring for bloom the following year; do not cover it. Rich soil and sun give best results. Many nurseries supply young plants each spring. Canterbury-bells and Madonna lilies seem made to go together, in the garden and as cut flowers.

C. *persicifolia*
peach-leaved bellflower   2½ to 3 feet

PERENNIAL. This is valuable for color in the June flower border. Many spikes of white or blue flowers rise above the cushions of pointed leaves. They combine well with coralbells, peonies, gaillardia, and sweet-William (as illustrated) and other early June perennials. Scattered bloom continues through July. Plant in rich garden soil and full sun. Divide every third year Walter Haring photo

119

CARYOPTERIS *clandonensis*
blue-mist-flower, hardy blue-spirea
2½ to 3 feet

SHRUB. Low-growing shrubs with blue
flowers are few. Here is an enchanting
one, 'Heavenly Blue', with gray-green foliage and clusters of lilac-blue flowers on
slender stems, produced from August until
hard frost. It is attractive in front of foundation plantings or evergreen shrubs, or for
accent in the border. Plant in rich soil and
full sun. Sometimes caryopteris winterkills
but grows up quickly from soil level. It
combines beautifully with all late-summer
flowers. The Wayside Gardens Co. photo

CENTAUREA *cyanus*
bachelor's-button, cornflower
15 inches to 3 feet

ANNUAL. One of the very few really rich-
blue flowers and known to everyone, the
cornflower is a joy to have in the garden
and easy to grow. The foliage is gray-
green; the stems are long, as if made for
cutting. There are also pink and white varieties. Sow the seed in fertile but light soil
in sun and in late fall for early-summer
bloom. Plants resent transplanting; therefore sow where they are to grow. C. *mos-
chata*, 'Sweet Sultan', grows to 3 feet tall
and produces larger, very double, and fragrant flowers of pinkish-lavender or pale
yellow. If seed is not allowed to form,
flowers keep coming for weeks. Sow where
it is to grow in May. Both kinds are attractive with marigolds, zinnias, petunias, or
salpiglossis. Walter Haring photo

120

CERATOSTIGMA *larpentiae*
plumbago   8 to 10 inches

PERENNIAL. This hardy creeping plant is fine for rockeries if controlled or for ground-cover in sizable areas. The August and September flowers are about ¾ inch across and dark blue. Vigorous in any soil, in sun or part shade, this is tough enough even for city gardens. Foliage turns red in the fall, and does not show new growth until mid-May. Spring bulbs can be interplanted to furnish color and green before the plumbago leaves appear. A. B. Morse Company photo

CHIONODOXA *luciliae*
glory-of-the-snow   3 to 10 inches

BULB. Nothing in the early spring garden is so enchanting as a mass of chionodoxa. Up-facing blue or blue-violet, white-eyed flowers combine beautifully with early daffodils and species tulips. In drifts in the rock garden, along semishaded walks, at the foot of walls, under shrubs, they paint year after year unforgettable pictures. Plant 3 inches deep in any good soil in September, and replant every third or fourth year. The bulbs should not be kept out of the soil for long. In woodland settings they self-sow and perpetuate themselves for a lifetime. The form *gigantea* is illustrated. W. Atlee Burpee Co. photo

CLEMATIS   4 to 12 feet

VINE. This gorgeous vine is greatly admired wherever it can be grown. Clematis is reliably hardy except in the Upper North where temperatures regularly drop to below zero, and even there it is hardy in a protected spot. *Clematis jackmani purpurea* (right), blooming in early summer, is the best known. The flowers are 3 to 6 inches across. Others of this type have flowers of pale blue, lavender, pink, rose, and white (below right). The picture shows a few of these large-flowered hybrids. Others are illustrated in the sections on pink flowers and on white flowers. *C. paniculata* is covered with tiny white flowers in late summer and is excellent to cover old walls or fences. Use special care in planting. Select a spot where tops will be in the sun, roots in shade. Dig a large hole at least 15 inches deep, mixing the old soil with peatmoss and a cupful of lime. Young shoots need support to climb and this support should be placed when planting. Set the crown 2 inches below the soil surface. Water deeply and then spread a 1- to 2-inch permanent mulch. Fertilize yearly with dried cow manure and superphosphate, and work in wood ashes from the fireplace if you have them. Each fall, stir in a cupful of lime, unless your soil is highly alkaline. Water well if the summer is at all dry. Clematis takes a year or two to become established. *C. jackmani*, The Wayside Gardens Co. photo; hybrids, George W. Park Seed Co., Inc., photo

CYNOGLOSSUM *amabile*
Chinese forget-me-not   15 to 24 inches

ANNUAL. Starting to bloom in late July from May-sown seed, cynoglossum is easily grown and blends well with most other annuals. It is also delightful in large plantings near summer roses or, as here, with the yellow Dahlberg daisy. Sky-blue flowers are borne in sprays over velvety gray-green foliage. Sow the seed where plants are to bloom, in rich, moist soil. Transplanted seedlings will wilt badly for several days but will recover. George W. Park Seed Co., Inc., photo

DELPHINIUM
larkspur   2½ to 6 feet

PERENNIAL. In regions of cool summers delphiniums are long-lived, but in most sections of the country they live only two to four years. Purchased plants are not usually as strong as those grown from seed in the spring and set in their permanent places when 5 to 6 inches tall. Plant in rich moist soil, the crowns at soil level. Feed in spring with dried cow manure and superphosphate. Stake the flower spikes to prevent wind breakage. The Giant Pacific Hybrids (illustrated) come in many shades of blue, pink, lilac, and white. Blackmore and Langdon Hybrids have enormous flowers but tend to be only biennial. Connecticut Yankees are more shrubby, send up many airy flower spikes, and are longer lived than the large-flowered hybrids. They bloom all summer if spent flower stalks are removed. Often grown as an annual, *D. chinensis* is a graceful border plant, 2 to 3 feet high, with more delicate foliage and loose open spikes of gentian-blue flowers in June and July.

123

D. *ajacis*   3 to 4 feet

ANNUAL. Spectacular blue, white, or pink flowers stand up in tall spires above finely divided foliage. The seed needs cool weather for good germination, hence is best planted in the fall where plants are to grow. But it may be sown in early spring and again in late June for fall bloom. The flowering period runs from six to eight weeks. Plant in rich, moist soil and full sun, but this larkspur does not like summer heat and a situation providing some shade in the hottest part of the day would be ideal. With Shirley poppies it creates a delightful picture. George J. Ball, Inc., photos

DIDISCUS (*Trachymene*) *caerulea*
blue-lace-flower   1½ to 2 feet

ANNUAL. Rather like an azure or powder-blue Queen-Anne's-lace, this flower blends well with virtually every other in the garden, contributing a delicate filmy quality. Seed sown in May will yield long-stemmed flowers from July until frost, excellent for cutting. For earlier bloom start the seed indoors in March. Too pale to compete with vivid flowers, it is lovely with anthemis, pale yellow or white snapdragons, baby's-breath, or sea-lavender—either in the garden or in bouquets. W. Atlee Burpee Co. photo

ERYNGIUM *amethystinum*
    sea-holly   2½ to 3 feet

PERENNIAL. Eryngium has coarse serrated
leaves, branching stems, and large thimbles
of aggregated small flowers in blue or light
violet. In some forms the color is very pale
but the effect is lovely. Each flower-head
is surrounded at the base by large decorative bracts of gray-green, silver, or metallic
blue. It needs sun for at least half of the
day. Mature plants resent transplanting
George W. Park Seed Co., Inc., photo

EUPATORIUM *coelestinum*
    mist-flower, hardy ageratum   3 to 4 feet

PERENNIAL. One of the most satisfactory
plants for beds or borders in late summer
and early fall, eupatorium has long sturdy
stems which branch into umbels of fluffy
azure-blue or lavender flowers. Along the
edges of woodland walks or of borders it
will self-sow. It demands no special soil or
care other than sun for most of the day.
Growth does not show until mid-May, so
the location should be well marked to
avoid damage from early cultivation. The
Wayside Gardens Co. photo

125

EUTOCA *campanularia*
bee's-friend, California bluebell   1 foot

ANNUAL. It is strange that this easily grown plant, which rivals the difficult gentians for pure deep blue, is rather seldom seen in our gardens. The foliage is excellent, the habit dense and spreading, and in midsummer every stem produces several wide up-facing bells with snow-white anthers. In the variety 'Musgrave' the center is white. Few annuals create a more colorful carpet or edging in full sunshine. Seed can be sown outdoors in mid-May, but heat is needed for germination, and better results and earlier bloom are achieved by sowing indoors in April. Any well-drained garden soil is satisfactory. Petunias, sweet-alyssum, and dwarf marigolds will accentuate its vivid color. Eutoca is sometimes sold as Phacelia or Whitlavia, which are simply other names for it. George W. Park Seed Co., Inc., photo

HELIOTROPIUM *arborescens*
heliotrope, cherry-pie   1½ to 2½ feet

ANNUAL. Much in vogue in great-grandmother's day, heliotrope bears fragrant lavender or purple blooms in coiled racemes. Formerly a favorite for solid bed plantings, it is fine also in the border. Plant in rich moist soil and full sun. Named varieties include 'Blue Bonnet' and 'Marine'. Combines well with white or pink petunias. George W. Park Seed Co., Inc., photo

IRIS

½ to 4 feet

PERENNIAL. The majority of this extensive genus consists of very hardy and enduring plants with rhizomatous roots, sword-shaped leaves, and rigid stems bearing showy flowers of exquisite texture and brilliant color. May and early June is the season for most, the Japanese kinds in late June and early July. The tall bearded group (right) is the familiar "German" iris, actually now hybrids of many species. These include dwarfs (below right), medium-height, and tall ones. Any fertile soil with reasonable drainage and sunny exposure suits them. Rhizomes should be set just below the soil surface, where after blooming they like to be dry and warm. Divide the clumps, with a sharp knife, every third year in August. The beardless group contains the familiar Siberian iris, with taller, thinner, more graceful leaves and slightly smaller flowers. They need the same cultivation. The tall Japanese iris (*I. kaemferi*) have immense, flat flowers, and need a heavier soil, even clay, completely lime-free, and abundant moisture. The similar, more refined *I. laevigata* likes a very wet situation all year round at the edge of a pond.

BULBOUS. A third group, the bulbous iris, is mostly low-growing. The purple *I. reticulata* and yellow *I. danfordiae* may bloom in a sheltered south-facing place the first week of March. These are well suited to the rock garden, and also make charming house plants. For mid-May and early June are the so-called Dutch, Spanish, and English iris, with exquisite flowers on 18-inch stems. Schreiner's Gardens, Salem, Oregon, photos

Japanese iris (top left) and Siberian iris (top right), Walter Haring photos; Spuria iris (bottom left), Schreiner's Gardens, Salem, Oregon, photo; and Dutch iris 'Imperator' (bottom right), W. Atlee Burpee Co. photo

LAVANDULA *officinalis*
lavender   1½ to 2 feet

SHRUB. Well-known for its clean fragrance, sweet lavender is a dwarf shrub excellent for beds and borders, for patterns in the herb garden, and for low hedges. In July and August the tiny flowers are borne in spikes above cool gray-green foliage. Light soil and sun are essential for success. In severe winters tops may winterkill but fresh growth comes up from the crown in spring. The planting should be renewed every four or five years. A. B. Morse Company photo

LIATRIS
gayfeather   3 to 5 feet

PERENNIAL. Although they vary and there are white ones, the usual color of liatris is close to magenta. Many flowers are borne on narrow spikes above thick tufts of grassy leaves in late summer. Unusual and striking, they are dependable even in dry places, do well in city gardens, and really flourish in rich soil and part shade. By ponds they sometimes naturalize. Pink or white phlox and other plants in any color except red accord with them. Their strong stems make them satisfactory and showy cut flowers. A. B. Morse Company photo

129

LIMONIUM *latifolium*
 sea-lavender   1 to 2½ feet

PERENNIAL. Clouds of small rosy-purple flowers like those of *Gypsophila* cover the delicate branching stems of these plants in late summer and early fall. The leaves are basal only and rather large. Of easiest culture in rich soil and sun, sea-lavender will bloom for weeks. The Wayside Gardens Co. photo

L. *sinuatum*
 statice   15 to 18 inches

ANNUAL. On the shores of the Mediterranean this plant is perennial. Not hardy north, it will fortunately grow as an annual with us. The branching heads of papery violet, white, or pale yellow flowers open from July to frost. Seed may be sown outdoors where plants are to grow in rich soil and full sun, or for earlier bloom indoors in February or March, to be transplanted in May. Statice is excellent for accent in beds and borders and colorful in dried winter bouquets. W. Atlee Burpee Co. photo

LINUM *perenne*
blue flax   1 to 1½ feet

PERENNIAL. True heavenly blue is the color of these airy and distinctive flowers. The branching stems are slender, the upper part clothed with small light green leaves. Blue flax adds lightness and sparkle to the border on June and July mornings, its flowers closing shortly after noon. Any light rich soil will suit it, but it must have full sun. Lemon daylilies, coreopsis, iris, and columbine make charming effects with flax. A. B. Morse Company photo

LOBELIA *erinus*
blue lobelia   4 to 8 inches

ANNUAL. A popular edging plant, lobelia is also unsurpassed as a ground-cover and in the rockery. The cascade forms are fine in hanging baskets. The typical form has bright true blue flowers, small but very showy from June to frost. Lavender, white, pink, and magenta varieties are available. Lobelia seed is extremely small and easily washed away if planted directly in the garden. Sow it indoors in late February or March. Spoon up the tiny fragile seedlings in small bunches into flats or pots. When larger the young plants can be readily pulled apart and set outdoors in mid-May. Plant in sun or semishade in any garden soil. For best results set 4 to 6 inches apart. Shear them in midsummer to encourage further bloom. Combine with rose, pink, or red petunias, with dwarf marigolds and low-growing celosia. Combine with sweet-alyssum for a blue and white ground-cover. George J. Ball, Inc., photo

MAHONIA *aquifolium*
Oregon holly-grape   2 to 5 feet

SHRUB. This glossy evergreen has dark spiny leaves which turn bronze in winter. Chartreuse clustered flowers come in May, followed by effective blue or blue-black fruits, which make excellent jelly. It is a splendid shrub for north-facing foundations, but if exposed to late winter winds and sun, leaf burn will result, although new leaves rather quickly develop. In a sheltered location *M. bealei*, the leather-leaf-holly, is hardy as far north as New York. The flowers are pale yellow and sweet-scented. It does best in semishade. Both species should be watered copiously in time of drought. The Wayside Gardens Co. photo

MERTENSIA *virginica*
Virginia bluebell   1 to 2 feet

PERENNIAL. One of the best-loved of spring flowers, this is hardy and long-lived, in sun or shade. The nodding graceful clusters, rose-pink in bud, open to a lovely blue. The foliage dies down after blooming. Do not disturb established plants; if transplanting is necessary, do it only in the dormant period about midsummer. This is a lovely companion to daffodils, bleeding-hearts, and iberis and can be naturalized along shady brooks. A. B. Morse Company photo

MUSCARI
grape-hyacinth   5 to 8 inches

BULB. Known as "blue bells" in many sections of the country, these friendly little flowers have become as beloved as the crocus. They are unexcelled for color in the spring garden, especially when seen in close numbers. *M. botryoides* blooms with the crocus. *M. armeniacum* (illustrated) is larger flowered, the best for massing and opens just as the crocuses disappear. This is the species usually grown. Its white form is particularly fine. *M. comosum* var. *plumosum* is the plume-hyacinth, having unusual feathery flowers colored violet. Plant muscari as soon as the bulbs arrive in September, 3 inches deep in fertile well-drained soil. They are lovely everywhere, in the rockery, below banks or walls, in woodland, edging the border, and with tulips or early narcissus. Robert Miner photo

MYOSOTIS
forget-me-not   6 to 12 inches

BIENNIAL. *M. alpestris* (illustrated) is compact in habit with small blue flowers in clusters on downy foliage. It is a pleasing foil for spring bulbs. Sown in February indoors, it will bloom in May and continue for about six weeks. *M. palustris semperflorens,* which is perennial, grows taller on smoother foliage and also has pale blue flowers. This species is quite hardy, well-suited to moist semishaded areas, and naturalizes easily. Lovely effects are possible with either of these forget-me-nots and pansies, arabis, yellow alyssum, and tulips. Walter Haring photo

NEPETA *mussini*
catnip   1 to 1½ feet

PERENNIAL. There are a number of ne-
petas, but the best for color in the garden
is this species. The foliage is bushy, downy
gray-green, and aromatic; the lavender-blue
flowers appear profusely in June and then
lightly through the summer. It grows in
the poorest soil in my garden. And it needs
sun for a good part of the day. Most often
seen in herb gardens, it is lovely in masses
in the front of the border or along paved
walks. The soft foliage harmonizes with
any neighboring flowers. The Wayside
Gardens Co. photo

NIEREMBERGIA *caerulea*
cup-flower   6 to 8 inches

ANNUAL. Although perennial in protected
gardens, nierembergia is usually grown as
an annual in the North. It is a bushy little
plant with fine, close-set foliage and inch-
wide flowers, shallow cup-shaped, deep
blue or lavender. 'Purple Robe' is illustrated. In the border, in the rockery, or as
edging, it blooms for weeks in midsummer.
A most pleasing color scheme is with pink
or rose verbena or petunias. George J. Ball,
Inc., photo

134

NIGELLA *damascena*
  love-in-a-mist   15 inches

ANNUAL. Love-in-a-mist is a short-lived annual but distinct from all others. The foliage is threadlike, the light blue or lavender flowers surrounded by threadlike bracts, so that the whole effect is lacy and veil-like. The balloon-shaped seed pods are favorites for winter bouquets. Choose a sunny place where the soil is not heavy and sow the seed where it is to grow, for nigella does not transplant well. Nor does it remain long in flower, making more than one seed sowing desirable—about May 1 for blooms by July and in late June for fall bloom. The variety 'Miss Jekyll' has flowers of light blue. 'Persian Rose' has old-rose flowers, and *N. hispanica*, purple. George W. Park Seed Co., Inc., photo

PHLOX *divaricata*
  wild sweet-William   12 to 15 inches

PERENNIAL. A native plant of the Appalachians and Midwest, *Phlox divaricata* opens crowded clusters of lavender-blue flowers in May. In rich, moist soil in light shade it increases rapidly. Blue Phlox blends with primula, pulmonaria, late tulips, and daffodils. Walter Haring photo

135

PLATYCODON *grandiflorum*
balloon-flower   1 to 3 feet

PERENNIAL. These flowers are much like those of campanula but opening wider and not bell-shaped. The buds are little balloons. It is a hardy and satisfactory plant, flowering in July and then lightly until frost, especially if prevented from forming seed. It should be planted where it will not be disturbed for years in rich, friable soil and full sun. Since growth does not appear until mid-May, the location should be well marked so that crowns will not be damaged by early cultivation. The stems are somewhat soft and may well be tied to light stakes when a foot high. White Shasta daisy and yellow flowers are good companions. George W. Park Seed Co., Inc., photo

PULMONARIA
lungwort   8 to 10 inches

PERENNIAL. In early spring, these plants of European woodlands start to bloom when only 4 inches high, and their stems elongate as the season advances, lifting the later flowers high above the leaves. Pink buds open to blue flowers. The two-colored effect is lovely in itself or when enhanced by pink hyacinths and *Tulipa tarda* or a mass planting of rockcress. *P. angustifolia* has downy leaves and deep blue flowers; *P. saccharata*, sometimes called trout-plant or Bethlehem-sage, has gray-green leaves spotted white. Both species prefer a slightly shaded position in rich, moist soil. The Wayside Gardens Co. photo

SALPIGLOSSIS *sinuata*
    painted-tongue   2 to 3 feet

ANNUAL. Trumpet flowers in shades of rich red, garnet, rose, blue, yellow, and purple, usually with striped markings in the throat, open from July until frost. They have great sublety of coloring and exquisite form. The stems are wiry, and the flowers keep well in arrangements. When well grown this is an excellent garden subject; it blends with petunias, dwarf marigolds, feverfew, and the dusty millers, and is handsome with the Mexican tulip-poppy, *Hunnemannia*. Sow seeds indoors in March or directly in the garden in May. The very fine seed should be only scattered on the surface, not covered. Salpiglossis resents transplanting, except when very young. Plant in light, sandy soil and in full sun or light shade. W. Atlee Burpee Co. photo

SALVIA *farinacea*
    mealycup salvia   3 feet

PERENNIAL. This lovely salvia is not reliably hardy in the North, but easily grown from seed started indoors in late winter. 'Blue Bedder', a great favorite in our garden, blooms pleasingly with snapdragons, petunias, zinnias, and many other annuals. There is also a 'White Bedder'. Either variety makes a good accent plant throughout the perennial border. Here, it grows with dahlias and marigolds. Walter Haring photo

SCILLA *sibirica*
Siberian squill   4 to 6 inches

BULB. In April, right after the early crocus, come these lovely little nodding flowers, dark blue or azure, making pools of color under shrubs or in the rock garden, in front of early tulips, and effective with white hyacinths and the tiny early red *Tulipa praestans* 'Fusilier'. *S. hispanica*, the wood hyacinth, or Spanish bluebell, is taller, to 20 inches, later blooming—blue, pink, or white—and lovely at the end of May and in early June. Each stalk bears several flowers in a loose spike. Bulbs increase and endure for years and can be naturalized in woodland or thickly clustered at the edge of shrubbery. Walter Haring photo

SYRINGA
lilac   6 to 8 feet

SHRUB. The lilac so long a part of American tradition and sentiment, found in old farms and dooryards, is *S. vulgaris*. One reason it has survived there is because the farm soil was rich, all lilacs being heavy feeders and needing deep, rich soil and some lime to do their best. The large trusses of bloom are very fragrant and come in lovely shades of pale lavender to purple, early in May unless the spring is cold. Today there are many superior hybrids, foremost among them the French lilacs, which have deeper colors and larger clusters—blue-lavender to red-purple, white, or deep cream. Young plants take two to three years to become established and to produce abundant flowers. A yearly application of wood ashes and superphosphate in spring will keep them in good blooming condition. Coming with Darwin tulips and early iris, lilacs lend themselves to beautiful color schemes, the white lilacs particularly. The Wayside Gardens Co. photo

138

TORENIA *fournieri*
wishbone-flower   8 to 12 inches

ANNUAL. This is a dainty little plant with bronze foliage and short spikes of tubular flowers, blue and violet with a yellow throat. In the North it blooms from midsummer to frost. In frost-free areas it often substitutes for the pansy. Sow seed indoors in February or March, for torenia needs a long growing season to come into bloom. Plant in semishaded areas where soil is rich, deep, and moist. Try it with pink begonias or impatiens for a lovely picture in a partly shaded area. W. Atlee Burpee Co. photo

VERBENA *hortensis*
garden verbena   1 to 1½ feet

ANNUAL. Excellent for bedding, verbena has gray-green foliage topped with long-stemmed clusters of small florets in blue, purple, pink, red, or white, and some with white centers to each floret. Plant where it is to grow in May or sow seed indoors in March for earliest bloom. It flowers from July to hard frost, and most profusely in sun. This is a good plant for poor soil, even withstanding drought. Walter Haring photo

VERONICA
speedwell   6 inches to 3 feet

PERENNIAL. There are a number of veronicas for the perennial bed or border and several suitable for the rock garden. All need sun and good garden soil. *V. amethystinum* 'Royal Blue' (right), growing 10 to 15 inches high, blooms in June

and July. 'Crater Lake Blue' is especially beautiful and strong and hardy. *V. incana* has gray foliage and light blue flowers on 15-inch stems in May and June. *V. rupestris* is a lovely creeping plant suitable for the rockery with flowers of light blue. 'Icicle' (left), blooming from July to September, is an excellent white. All need plenty of water in dry weather. Walter Haring photo

VINCA *minor*
myrtle   3 inches

PERENNIAL. This creeper has small shiny evergreen leaves and lavender-blue flowers about 1 inch across in late spring and early summer. It is invaluable for ground-covers and on banks, especially in shade. Although needing a year or two to become established, it then grows quite rapidly in any good soil. 'Double Blue' is illustrated. *Vinca major* is not hardy north but is useful for window boxes. The Wayside Gardens Co. photo

VIOLA *tricolor hortensis*
pansy   6 to 10 inches

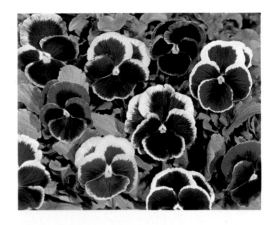

ANNUAL. The appealing pansy is known to everyone, and this variety, 'Bold Faces', is a darling. Pansies start to bloom in early spring with tulips and the first flowers of *Iberis sempervirens* and *Alyssum saxatile*. They are a joy anywhere—in the rockery, in beds with spring bulbs, and in borders. They thrive in sun or light shade, in rich soil well supplied with water. Faded blooms must be consistently removed if flowering is to continue for a long period. It may cease in hot weather but start again in the cooler weeks of fall if sprawling growth is cut back. Buy plants in spring or sow seed in August for bloom for next spring. There are wonderful varieties and colors for every garden. Where winters are mild, pansies may live over and even bloom in cold weather. The perennial sweet violet, *V. odorata,* is marvelously fragrant and blooms in spring and again in fall, large and lovely flowers in clear blue, dark purple, pink, old rose, and white, but plants are likely to be tender and rarely survive our cold winters. George J. Ball, Inc., photo

V. cornuta hybrids
viola, tufted pansy   6 inches

BIENNIAL. Violas are little plants with small pansy flowers borne profusely in early spring and lightly throughout the summer. Long ago, *V. cornuta* was crossed with *V. tricolor* to give fine large blossoms and a spectrum of hues—white, apricot, yellow, lavender, and dark purple. 'John Wallmark' is shown here. Violas thrive in semishade, rich cool soil, and plenty of moisture. Where winters are not too cold, they tend to be perennial but quickly die out in drought. If sown early indoors in March, they start to bloom in June. Johnny-jump-up is a diminutive viola that self-sows readily and appears unexpectedly in many places through summer and even into cold weather. The Wayside Gardens Co. photo

141

VITEX *macrophylla*
    chaste-tree   6 to 10 feet

SHRUB. This semihardy shrub produces a wealth of long spikes of leathery lavender flowers in July and continues for weeks. In colder areas it sometimes winter-kills but quickly grows again from the root. No special soil is needed. Vitex is used as a specimen shrub or as background in full sun or semishade. A. B. Morse Company photo

WISTERIA   12 to 40 feet

VINE. Here is the Chinese *W. sinensis,* the hardy deciduous climber of nostalgic association. Foot-long fragrant flowers, lavender or white, open from early- to mid-May and last two to three weeks, depending on weather. The whole cluster opens at once and ahead of the leaves. A mighty grower, wisteria twists and twines around supports and is not for a limited space; it can climb up a four-story house and may even pry off shingles, but it is handsome indeed for a large pergola or veranda, and preferably in full sun. A fertilizer low in nitrogen is best to stimulate flower rather than leaf production. Prune established vines heavily after blooming and cut back the long green side shoots to three eyes again in July and August. (New plants may not leaf out until August; meanwhile keep well watered.) If bloom is sparse on a young vine, root-prune 18 inches deep early in spring, cut back tops and fertilize with superphosphate; feed again in late fall, mulching the first year. Water deeply in dry weather. The Japanese *W. floribunda,* white and in shades of pink to purple in many fine named varieties, bears much longer chains, even to 6 feet. It is spectacular and hardy as far north as New Hampshire and Vermont. It blooms a little later than the Chinese, the florets opening from base to tip rather than all at once, and along with the new leaves. The Wayside Gardens Co. photo

'White Admiral' phlox with lythrum and daylilies in the author's garden.
Walter Haring photo.

WHITE AND GREEN

JUDICIOUSLY used, white either in the form of foliage or of bloom creates a cool and refreshing effect. The misty or frosty foliage of artemisia, santolina, and the dusty millers, the gray-greens of some geraniums, the blue-greens of rue and some hostas not only have interesting forms and textures but are most useful to separate strong colors and to modify the effect of companion plants of different colors, such as blue and yellow. White flowers, of course, accord with and enhance the color of any neighboring plants. They are also valuable in giving unity to a garden of many colors.

An interest in green flowers, perhaps primarily because of their rarity, has led to an increasing development of hybrids and varieties in that color. Recent years have seen introductions of green daylilies, true lilies, galdiolus, zinnia, nicotiana, and even a green-eyed gloriosa daisy. Most of these have a touch of chartreuse, resulting in a cool, delicate shade that blends well with blue, yellow, and white companion plants.

We are all aware of the wonderfully varied framework of green foliage with which nature has set off most flowering plants. A garden too needs this investiture of green, in trees, shrubs, and vines. The leaf color and texture of the background is as important as the color relation of flowers, and being of a more permanent nature, should always be borne in mind.

ABELIOPHYLLUM *distichum*
white-forsythia   3½ to 5 feet

SHRUB. In early spring the leafless branches of this shrub are covered with bell-shaped white flowers. Abeliophyllum is attractive as a specimen shrub or in mixed plantings, blooming two weeks ahead of forsythia. Where winters are mild it will bloom as early as February. In autumn, purple flower buds add beauty to the fall garden. Abeliophyllum is slow to become established and never grows really large; well suited to a small garden. Give it sun and rich soil. The Wayside Gardens Co. photo

ACIDANTHERA *bicolor*
peacock-orchid   2 to 3 feet

BULB. Often offered as *Gladiolus murieliae*, this plant has distinguished brown-centered white flowers. Four to six appear on each 2- to 3-foot stem in late summer. Not hardy in the North, it should not be set out there until danger of frost has passed. Any average good soil is acceptable. In late September or early October, lift the corms and store over winter like gladiolus. In full sun in clumps in the shrub or perennial border, it will thrive and blend well with most other flowers. Brown's Bulb Ranch photos

146

AMELANCHIER *asiatica*
shadbush, Juneberry   10 feet

SHRUB.   White flowers adorn the familiar
shadbush (*A. canadensis*) in late April or
early May. The leaves are a pleasing soft
green all summer. Equally hardy and even
finer in bloom is the Asian species, shown
here. It is a delightful small tree for woodland walks, or as a background for daffodils and early tulips, or above a carpet of
grape-hyacinths. It will grow in any soil in
sun or part shade. The fruit, resembling a
blueberry, ripens in June and attracts many
birds. The Wayside Gardens Co. photo

ANDROMEDA *catesbaei*
drooping leucothoe   2 to 3 feet

SHRUB.   This hardy broad-leaved evergreen, known also as Pieris, is a splendid
small shrub to face down plantings of rhododendron and azalea, to soften the foot of
rock walls, and to brighten woodland paths.
The leaves are attractive, deep shining
green, turning bronze in winter. The nodding white bell-flowers are borne on the
tips of the branches in early spring. Plant
andromeda in semishade in rich, peaty soil
and maintain a permanent mulch of leafmold or peat moss. Water plentifully in
time of drought. Walter Haring photo

147

ANTIRRHINUM *majus*
snapdragon   1½ to 3 feet

ANNUAL. Although snapdragons are perennial in mild climates, they are grown as annuals in most sections of the country. The pouch flowers are borne on long spikes from July to frost. Since a long growing season is needed to bloom, seed should be sown early indoors or in a cold frame. There are 6-inch dwarfs and varieties from 18 inches to 3 feet, in white and shades of yellow, orange, scarlet, pink, coral, and salmon. Plant in rich, moist soil in full sun or where there is sun at least for half of the day. The showy spikes of snapdragons are beautiful with asters, ageratum, marigolds, petunias, zinnias, and also with green nicotiana as here in the author's garden. Walter Haring photo

AQUILEGIA *flabellata nana*
dwarf Japanese columbine   1 foot

PERENNIAL. This columbine blooms in late April and early May. The foliage is of outstanding beauty, the short-spurred flowers pale blue in the type or pure white in *nana alba*. A fine plant for the rock garden or border, it is especially lovely interplanted with lavender *Phlox divaricata*. It grows easily in sun or part shade in rich garden soil. Seed sown early in spring produces bloom the second year. Walter Haring photo

ARABIS *albida*
rock-cress   6 inches

PERENNIAL. In late April, arabis produces quantities of pure white flowers in small loose clusters. It is a spreading plant for rockeries, edgings, and steep banks. The foliage is pubescent, gray-green. Plant in any garden soil in sun or part shade, and next to pansy, *Phlox subulata*, forget-me-nots, or grape-hyacinths for pleasing contrasts. Walter Haring photo

ARCTOTIS *grandis*
blue-eyed daisy   1 to 2 feet

ANNUAL. Arctotis is one of several annuals that are called African daisy. The species itself has white, 3-inch-wide flowers with a powder-blue center. Newer hybrids have flowers in shades of yellow, orange and red. They must have full sun and friable soil; are very good for hot, dry locations. Arctotis combines well with snapdragons, cynoglossum, and salvia 'Blue Bedder'. George W. Park Seed Co., Inc., photo

149

ARONIA *arbutifolia*
chokeberry   5 to 6 feet

SHRUB. Clusters of white flowers in May and red fruits and leaves in September make aronia a doubly valuable garden shrub. Upright growing, it is happy in sun or semishade and in any reasonably good soil. A hedge of *aronia* never needs shearing. Scattered plants are charming along shady paths. The bright fruits hang on all winter. The variety *erecta* (illustrated), being compact and narrow, is very good in a small garden. The Wayside Gardens Co. photo

ARTEMISIA
wormwood, southernwood   1 to 3 feet

PERENNIAL. The variety 'Silver King' (below left), often mistakenly called dusty miller, grows to 3 feet and has inconspicuous white flowers. *A. stellariana* grows to 18 inches with tiny yellow flowers. Both are cultivated for their finely cut gray foliage. 'Silver Mound' (below right) makes thick mats of blue-silver leaves, which can add interest to the rock garden. All like warm soil and much sun. Foliage and flowers are handsome in dried winter bouquets. Walter Haring photos

ASTILBE *japonica*   1½ to 2 feet

PERENNIAL. This is one of the best perennials for the flower border, having decorative compound foliage and erect plumelike panicles of showy white flowers in June. It must have rich garden soil plentifully supplied with moisture, in sun or semishade, and should be divided every three or four years. A group of hybrids, known as *A. arendsi*, have flowers also in rose, pink, carmine, and brilliant red. Walter Haring photo

BELLIS *perennis*
English daisy   6 inches

BIENNIAL. These charming little flowers of late April and early May will bloom the second year from spring-sown seed. But they are available wherever pansy plants are sold and are best used as an annual. The blossoms are usually double in white, pink, rose, or red. Satisfactory in light shade, they rejoice in rich, moist soil and sun. Always appealing with pansies and spring bulbs, they also make neat edgings or good groups in the rock garden. A. B. Morse Company photo

BERGENIA *cordifolia*   1 foot

PERENNIAL.   Often offered as Saxifraga, to which it is closely related, this plant produces handsome large leathery leaves and flowers of white or clear deep rose in clusters on strong stems. It is attractive in the rockery or as ground-cover under trees. Flowering time is April or early May. Moist woodsy soil and sun or semishade are right for bergenia. It also does well in shaded city gardens. A. B. Morse Company photo

CALADIUM *bicolor*   15 to 24 inches

TUBER.   In shade or semishade, the exotic foliage of caladium adds a special charm to any garden. The large decorative leaves are green and white or shades of cream, pink, and rose, edged or veined with green and white. Not winter hardy, the tubers must be dug after the foliage has begun to wither in the fall and stored in a warm place where they will not completely dry out. Start the tubers indoors in March, keep them at 75 degrees, and plant in the garden in late May in rich soil in shade or semishade. A. B. Morse Company photo

152

CHIONANTHUS *virginica*
fringe-tree, old-man's beard   10 to 20 feet

TREE. Seeming more shrubby than tree-like, this American plant is hardy as far north as Boston if given the shelter of a house or evergreen windbreak. It is cher-ished for its drooping panicles of fragrant greenish-white flowers in early June. Give it well-drained yet moist soil in light shade. The beautiful oblong leaves turn golden yellow in autumn. A. B. Morse Company photo

CHRYSANTHEMUM *maximum*
Shasta daisy   2 to 3 feet

PERENNIAL. To any garden these porcelain-white flowers bring sparkle. Single forms with yellow or vivid orange centers, double, and semidouble forms are available. In rich soil they bloom superbly through July and August. Give them room to accommodate their branching habit. Lift and divide the clumps every fall if possible. Striking schemes can be worked out with monarda 'Cambridge Red', helianthus, heliopsis, delphinium, and hemerocallis, and refreshing, unusual effects with other white flowers and gray-leaved plants. Walter Haring photo

153

CINERARIA *maritima*
dusty miller   12 to 15 inches

ANNUAL. Two outstanding varieties of dusty miller are 'Diamond' and 'Silver Queen', which is illustrated. Both are grown as annuals in the North, and provide excellent foliage contrast in beds and borders. Full sun and rich soil are needed to grow them well. 'Diamond' has spectacular white foliage with small inconspicuous yellow flowers. 'Silver Queen' has leaves like silvery filigree. It is lower growing and uniform in stature, making a fine edging for petunias, ageratum, phlox, anchusa 'Blue Bird', snapdragons, and geraniums. Walter Haring photo

CLEMATIS *jackmani*
hybrids   to 8 feet

VINE. This name covers a group of large-flowered hybrids which bloom variously from early to late summer, on the current year's growth. They should be pruned back rather heavily when dormant. For general culture of clematis see page 122. The many showy varieties include 'Nelly Moser', palest mauve with red bands, 'W. E. Gladstone', blue-lavender, and 'Henryi' (illustrated). Walter Haring photo

COLEUS *blumei*
flame-nettle   1 to 3 feet

ANNUAL.   Perennial in its native Java, this exotic if familiar plant is grown as an annual in our gardens and window boxes. The leaves are gorgeously colored and marked in rose, red, purple, and cream, varying greatly on individual plants, as in the rock-wall picture. The cool green-and-white strain (Master Blends Rainbow from Sakata) looks particularly attractive on a hot summer day. Coleus grows well under trees or shrubs where most other annuals will not thrive. The flowers are dull lavender spikes; they should be picked off as soon as they show. In rich, moist soil in semishade the leaves hold their colors until frost. Plants can be raised from spring-sown seed in the usual way, or from tip cuttings of older plants. When plants are about 6 inches high, pinch out tops to make them branch. Begonias and impatiens enjoy the same conditions and provide interesting contrasts of form and texture. Walter Haring photos

CONVALLARIA *majalis*
lily-of-the-valley   6 to 10 inches

PERENNIAL. Long cherished for its pervasive fragrance, lily-of-the-valley blooms in May with the lilacs. It grows from a horizontal rootstock from which develops a bud or "pip"—the part planted in early spring. Racemes of small nodding flowers on short stalks rise from light green basal foliage. Lily-of-the valley will grow in sun but does best on the north side of buildings or under deciduous trees in rich, moist soil. The roots become densely entwined and should be divided every third year. George W. Park Seed Co., Inc., photo

CORNUS *florida*
flowering dogwood   20 feet

TREE. This beautiful May-flowering tree (illustrated) is hardy as far north as Boston. The true flowers are clusters of little florets, the apparent "flowers" are the surrounding four large white bracts. In the fall the foliage turns scarlet and is interspersed with numerous red berries. Dogwood is easy to grow and long-lived. Plant it in sun and in rich soil plentifully supplied with moisture in time of drought. Fertilize in spring and fall with shredded dried cow manure and bonemeal. A permanent mulch of fir-bark or peatmoss is beneficial. *Cornus kousa*, the Korean dogwood, is similar but the flowers are flatter and are produced in profusion in June. The red fruits in fall resemble raspberries. A. B. Morse Company photo

DATURA *meteloides*
angel's-trumpet, moonflower   3 to 5 feet

ANNUAL. This lovely flower, grown as an annual in the North, is perennial in areas of milder winters. If heavily mulched, it sometimes survives northern winters. The foliage is a soft, velvety gray-green; the flowers are large open trumpets of pure white, and appear all summer. Sow seed where it is to grow in May in any good soil in full sun. Datura is handsome with salvia 'Blue Bedder' and with marigolds or dahlias. Walter Haring photo

DICTAMNUS *albus*
gas-plant   2 to 3 feet

PERENNIAL. A beautiful long-lived perennial, dictamnus has gray-green foliage; in May it has racemes of white flowers. The variety *rubra* has rose-purple flowers. This plant should never be moved once it has become established. It will flourish for years in rich, moist soil with at least six hours of sun each day. To add to its virtues, dictamnus needs no winter protection and harmonizes with all other May flowers. Walter Haring photo

EREMURUS
foxtail-lily
3 to 6 feet

PERENNIAL. The curious root of this plant looks like a bulb with thick rhizomes radiating from it. The tall flower spikes are effective in the background of the perennial border and magnificent in a bed by themselves. Leaves are basal and numerous; stems bear hundreds of tiny feathery flowers, ranging from pink to lavender, white, and yellow. They appear in June and July and go on for many weeks, after which the foliage tends to die down. Roots are brittle and must be planted carefully, in September and October, spread gently and covered with 4 to 5 inches of soil. Plant where they can remain undisturbed for years in full sun in deep rich soil and give a mulch of at least 6 inches of peatmoss for winter, removing the mulch in spring but not until the weather is settled, as new growth starts very early and can be killed by late frost. The Shelford Hybrids are very fine. A. B. Morse Company photo

EUPHORBIA *marginata*
snow-on-the-mountain
2 to 3 feet

ANNUAL. The succulent light green leaves of this plant are edged with white and the minute flowers are surrounded by showy large leaflike bracts of white or white and green. Doing well in poor soils, it will grow quite lush and tall in rich garden soil and six hours of sun a day. Vigorous and trouble-free, there is no plant that will so easily provide a marked contrast of foliage in beds and borders, looking cool in hot weather, and setting off all bright-colored flowers. Bodger Seeds, Ltd., photo

EXOCHORDA
pearl-bush   4 to 6 feet

SHRUB. Pearl-bush is a very hardy and graceful small shrub bearing snow-white flowers in great profusion in late April or early May. The flowers are followed by interesting winged seed-pods which are excellent for dried bouquets. E. *racemosa* grows to 6 feet. E. *macrantha* is more compact to 4 feet and beautifully suited to the small garden. 'The Bride' is illustrated. They accept any good soil in sun or light shade. The Wayside Gardens Co. photo

FRITILLARIA
guinea-hen flower, crown imperial
15 inches to 3 feet

BULB. Two forms are very hardy and long-lived. F. *meleagris* (illustrated), the guinea-hen flower, grows 15 to 18 inches tall with drooping bell-shaped flowers in curious shadings and frecklings of purple and white. F. *imperialis* is tall and stately when in bloom, the strong stalks surmounted by a whorl of leaves above an umbrella of bell flowers, brick-red, orange, or yellow. The lower leaves are large and bold, and have a definite skunk-cabbage odor. Plant the bulbs early in autumn in half-shade in rich soil and provide a deep mulch in winter in colder sections. Both species bloom in late April or May and can create interesting combinations with tulips and daffodils. W. Atlee Burpee Co. photo

GALANTHUS *nivalis*
snowdrop   6 to 8 inches

BULB. Before there are any other signs of spring, the delightful snowdrops push through the soil, sometimes even through melting snow. They are nodding white bells on slender stems. There is a variety with double flowers. Plant the small bulbs in fall under trees and shrubs or at the foot of rocks, any place where a few bulbs may be left undisturbed. In cool, moist soil they will increase every year. When planted thickly they make a glorious effect. Walter Haring photo

GYPSOPHILA
baby's-breath   1 to 4 feet

PERENNIAL AND ANNUAL. These old-fashioned plants are still treasured for their clouds of small white flowers and delicate foliage. The perennial *G. paniculata* is long-lived in a well-limed soil with plenty of watering in summer. Being tap-rooted, it should be planted where it is to remain, in any soil and full sun. Some varieties grow to 4 feet high and 4 feet across, making effective mounds. They tend to sprawl and should be staked. Variety *compacta* and variety 'Bristol Fairy' with double flowers grow about 2 feet high and are better for the small garden, as is the dwarf

G. repens (illustrated). These sorts bloom in June and July. 'Pink Fairy' and 'Pink Star' bloom from June to late summer. Baby's-breath is useful for hiding the fading foliage of Oriental poppy and bleeding-heart and concealing the bare spots which these plants leave. The annual baby's-breath, *G. elegans*, is easily grown from seed planted directly in the garden in May. It is lower growing, from 15 to 18 inches, and comes quickly into flower, but does not bloom for long, so it is well to sow again in late June and July. It is equally useful for filling in gaps left by earlier-flowering plants. The Wayside Gardens Co. photo

HALESIA *carolina*
silver-bell   20 to 30 feet

Tree. In May the arching branches of this small tree are hung with quantities of white bell-shaped flowers. Though not considered reliably hardy north of Philadelphia, it is not uncommonly found growing well as far north as Boston, particularly in rich, moist soil. It is delightful in a small garden. The Wayside Gardens Co. photo

HELLEBORUS
Christmas-rose, Lenten-rose   1 to 1½ feet

Perennial. Unfortunately this beautiful and hardy perennial is not widely grown. *H. niger* (illustrated) sometimes blooms as early as Christmas, hence its name. It has divided, evergreen, basal leaves and white flowers sometimes tinged with pink, 2½ to 3 inches across. *H. orientalis,* the Lenten-rose, blooms in spring. Its evergreen leaves are dotted with purple, its flowers dark purple outside and white within. There is a beautiful pink form. Both species need moisture and a deep rich soil, in a place partly shaded by other plants. A mulch of 2 or 3 inches of leafmold or peatmoss is desirable. Both species resent transplanting, even when young, but once established are hardy and long-lived. The Wayside Gardens Co. photo

161

HOSTA
plaintain-lily   2 to 3 feet

PERENNIAL. Hosta, formerly called Funkia, is one of the finest of hardy plants to use en masse in shade. Most species suffer in full sun but will tolerate about four hours of sun daily. Flowers are white or lavender and come in late summer. *H. glauca* or *sieboldiana* has most beautiful blue-green leaves and in June pale violet flowers. *H. lancifolia* has pinkish-lavender flowers; *H.* 'Thomas Hogg', handsome green leaves with a white margin; *H. variegata*, wavy-edged green-and-white leaves; and *H. ventricosa* vivid blue flowers. *H. decorata* is illustrated here. A unique species with large veined leaves and fragrant white flowers to 5 inches long is the August-lily, *H. subcordata*. Hostas like a rich moist soil. Without ample watering in hot weather, the leaves are apt to burn at the edges. Walter Haring photo

HYDRANGEA   3 to 6 feet

SHRUB. The old-fashioned *Hydrangea paniculata* is still widely grown for its huge panicles of flowers in late summer. It is most lovely when allowed to grow naturally and in association with other shrubs. The variety *praecox* (below) blooms six weeks earlier. *H. arborescens* 'Annabelle' (below right), a new form, is popular for hedges. *H. petiolaris* is a climber to 20 feet. All of these are hardy and strong-growing in any soil in sun or very light shade. *H. hortensis* or *H. opuloides*, the so-called florist's hydrangea, is not reliably hardy in the North except in protected gardens, but new plants can be purchased each spring and grow fast to 2 or 3 feet high. They are often used in tubs. The flowers tend to be pink in alkaline soil and blue in acid soil. The Wayside Gardens Co. photos

IBERIS *sempervirens*
hardy candytuft   10 to 12 inches

PERENNIAL. In May when late daffodils and tulips are in flower, the candytuft makes spreading mounds of sparkling white. Later the dense tiny leaves are evergreen. No plant is more useful for the edges of beds and borders and rock gardens, enhancing the colors of other flowers. With the blue of grape-hyacinth it makes an unforgettable spring picture. Iberis is hardy and long-lived but if not protected will die back in near zero weather with no snow. Plant it in full sun and rich soil. George W. Park Seed Co., Inc., photo

IPOMOEA *noctiflora*
moonvine, moonflower   10 feet

VINE. The "night-blooming morning glory" is a perennial in the South but grown as an annual in the North. It needs a long warm summer to mature. Sow seed indoors in moist vermiculite in April, at about 70 degrees. Planted out in late May, the vines grow fast, and climb by twisting stems. Leaves are very large, arrow shaped or sometimes three-lobed. On August evenings the large white flowers open almost suddenly and continue to come until frost. Moonvine needs rich soil and ample watering. Full sun is preferable and sun for at least half the day is essential. George W. Park Seed Co., Inc., photo

163

ISMENE *calathina*
Peruvian-daffodil   1½ to 2 feet

BULB. This exotic flower gives distinction to the garden in early summer, and later its lush leaves are attractive. Plant the large bulb just under the surface in May, in good soil well supplied with moisture and in a sunny location. The bold strap-like foliage will appear in a week or ten days and the blooms in four weeks from the day of planting. Three or more cream-white flowers open on each stem, the corolla edge fringed, as in the cultivar 'Avalanche' shown here. Bulbs should be lifted just before frost with roots and foliage attached. When the foliage turns yellow, remove it and store the bulbs in a warm place (at least 60 degrees) during winter. Open-mesh orange bags are good storage receptacles. Walter Haring photo

LEUCOJUM *vernum*
spring snowflake   8 to 12 inches

BULB. These green-tipped nodding white flowers resemble the snowdrop but are larger. Blooming with crocus and early tulips they add a much lighter and more delicate note. Plant them in early fall 3 inches deep and 3 inches apart in sun or semishade. If your garden site is hot and dry in the summer, find the coolest spot for these plants. A. B. Morse Company photo

LOBULARIA
sweet-alyssum   3 to 6 inches

ANNUAL. A favorite annual with all gardeners, sweet-alyssum has many uses—as a border plant, as an edging, in rockeries or as ground-cover. It will bloom all summer if lightly sheared after the first burst of bloom. The sprays of tiny white flowers on creeping foliage are very fragrant. 'Little Gem' and 'Carpet of Snow' (illustrated with Petunia 'Touché') are good varieties. For pink or lavender there are 'Royal Carpet', 'Violet Queen', 'Pink Heather', and 'Rosie O'Day'. Plant sweet-alyssum in any good soil and full sun. It goes charmingly with petunias, zinnias, verbena, geranium, marigold, snapdragon, and nasturtium. George J. Ball, Inc., photo

LUNARIA
honesty   2 to 3 feet

BIENNIAL. The four-petaled flowers of lunaria are attractive enough, if a little harsh, in lavender, purple, or white. It is the papery, shiny seed-pods for which the plants are generally grown and from which it is named. The pods are flat and moon-shaped, used in winter bouquets. Seed should be sown in spring in rather poor soil in sun or shade. W. Atlee Burpee Co. photo

165

MATHIOLA *incana*
stock   1 to 2 feet

ANNUAL. Though best known as a florist's flower, stocks can be grown as annuals in the North, and as biennials or perennials in warmer climes. The well-known Ten Weeks Mixed is illustrated. Fragrant flowers are borne in long spikes excellent for cutting. Pink, yellow, and purple forms are available as well as white. Sow seed early indoors or in covered frames in early March at a temperature of 65 degrees or lower. In order for them to set buds, the small plants should be grown at a temperature of 60 degrees. If summers are very hot, they may make large rosettes of leaves but produce few flowers. Set the young plants in deep, rich, moist soil and full sun. Attractive combinations are with larkspur, heliotrope, cosmos, or zinnias. Bodger Seeds, Ltd., photo

MATRICARIA
feverfew   8 inches to 2 feet

ANNUAL. Although perennial in protected gardens, matricaria is usually grown as annual in the North. The foliage is finely cut and the flowers are little daisies about ¾ inch across, single or double in white, yellow, cream. Sow the seed in rich soil in full sun, or indoors in March for earlier bloom. Where it is perennial it goes well with yellow foxglove and coralbells. When used as an annual, it combines beautifully with the later-flowering ageratum, dwarf marigolds, scarlet sage, salpiglossis, or annual phlox. Walter Haring photo

166

MOLUCELLA *laevis*
bells-of-Ireland   2 to 3 feet

ANNUAL. Grown for flower arrangements or in the green and white garden, bells of Ireland is a most unusual plant. Spikes of green bell-like "flowers" in whorls stand high above the rounded leaves. The actual flowers are tiny, white, and two-lipped. The showy part is a greatly enlarged green calyx. Though florists force them for spring bloom, in the garden they bloom from late July on. Seed should not be sown until the soil and air temperatures have warmed up to 70 degrees, usually toward the end of May. Germination takes 12 to 20 days. A rich, moist soil and full sun are best. For arrangements the leaves are removed and the stems conditioned in warm water in a cool place overnight. W. Atlee Burpee Co. photo

NARCISSUS   10 to 20 inches

BULB. Description and comment on this genus of plants is given in the "Yellow to Orange" section of this book. To many people the white species and varieties, especially the shallow-cupped sorts, seem quite different from yellow daffodils; and they do make a different and superlative effect in the spring garden. Named kinds can be had to bloom from early April until mid-May. All will increase from year to year and can be naturalized or grown in beds and borders, as in these two pictures from Helen Van Pelt Wilson's Connecticut garden. Robert Miner photos

NICOTIANA *alata*
ornamental tobacco   2½ to 4 feet

ANNUAL.   For its strong fragrance at night,
nicotiana should be in every garden, particularly near a veranda or window. The foliage, mostly basal, is large and velvety
gray-green. The flowers are borne from late
June to October. Rose, fuchsia, lavender,
and dark red varieties are available in dwarf
as well as tall varieties. This is a perennial
in frost-free areas but readily grown as an
annual throughout the United States, and
it self-sows freely. 'Daylight' has pure white
flowers; the 'Lime Sherbet' (illustrated) is
a lovely chartreuse, and grows to about 3
feet. Sow the seed in May where plants
are to grow in full sun and any good soil.
Don't cover the seed, merely press it gently
into moist soil. Germination takes place in
fourteen days. Young plants should be
thinned out when quite small, as they will
not transplant well later. Walter Haring
photo

ORNITHOGALUM *umbellatum*
star-of-Bethlehem   6 to 10 inches

BULB.   Originally from Mediterranean regions, these plants have become naturalized
in our northeastern states, and are charming when scattered in shaded rock gardens
or wild gardens. In late spring and early
summer they have branching corymbs of
six-petaled flowers, white inside and green
margined with white outside. The leaves
are grasslike, about 10 inches long. Plant
the bulbs in early fall 3 inches deep in good
soil. Once planted they will live for years.
P. deJager & Sons, Inc., photo

OXYDENDRUM *arboreum*
sorrel-tree, sourwood   15 to 30 feet

TREE. Interesting for its white flowers in July, its scarlet autumn color, and its small size, here is a valuable tree for yard and garden which is only beginning to be much used. It has a character all of its own. Though slow growing, it does well on the edges of woods and in city gardens and makes a decorative specimen. Bugs and blight do not bother it, and all kinds of soil will grow it, though one enriched with peatmoss, in sun or part shade, is preferred. A. B. Morse Company photo

PETUNIA *hybrida*
petunia   10 to 18 inches

ANNUAL. White petunias are among the most effective annuals for bedding in the summer garden. They bloom through summer and up to frost and combine beautifully with all colors. In this formal garden at the Powell-Waller house in Williamsburg, Va., white petunias are well used, with pink geraniums for accent. Colonial Williamsburg photo

PHILADELPHUS *lemoinei*
mock-orange   3 to 6 feet

SHRUB. The mock-oranges are covered with lovely waxy white flowers in June, filling the garden with a heavenly fragrance. Once planted in full sun and any good soil, they need no further care. 'Innocence' (illustrated) and 'Enchantment' have beautifully formed flowers. 'Belle Etoile' is double. There are lower-growing varieties for small areas. The Wayside Gardens Co. photo

POLYGONUM *auberti*
silver-lace-vine   15 to 20 feet

VINE. In late summer, yard-long sprays of tiny white fragrant flowers reach far out from this vigorous plant, probably the fastest-growing vine outside of the tropics. It will grow 10 feet or so the first season and to 40 feet eventually. Strong supports and vigilant trimming are needed. To bloom extravagantly it demands no special soil or care other than copious watering in dry weather and a sunny place. Pergolas, lattices, and sheds are turned into bowers. But keep it away from balconies and open porches if you are a tidy person, for it sheds leaves in dry weather, though without impairing its beauty. A. B. Morse Company photo

PUSCHKINIA *scilloides*
striped squill   6 inches

BULB. This charming little spring flower
is prized for the rock garden. The slender
stalk is topped with a raceme of hyacinth-
shaped florets of white striped with blue or
lavender. In any good soil, not heavy, in
sun or part shade, it will thrive and increase. To plantings of crocus and grape-
hyacinth it adds a note of different color
and form. Variety *libanotica,* with larger
individual flowers, is shown here. P. de-
Jager & Sons, Inc., photo

RUTA *graveolens*
herb-of-grace, rue   18 to 24 inches

PERENNIAL. The blue-green finely cut foliage of rue adds character to the flower
border, cools down clashing colors of neighboring flowers, and provides an oft-needed
contrast in the all green and white garden.
Some forms have bluer foliage than others,
'Blue Beauty' and 'Jackman's Blue' being
two. The yellow flowers are rather insig-
nificant and do not stay long. Rue likes
rich soil on the lime side, in sun or half
shade. The Wayside Gardens Co. photo

171

SEMPERVIVUM
hens-and-chicks   4 to 6 inches

PERENNIAL. These succulent plants are valued chiefly for their foliage. The leaves are tightly packed in rosettes, which in summer send up thick, 6- to 8-inch stems bearing crowded flowers of pink or rose. Around the original plant and nestling very close come the fat little chicks of new rosettes. The foliage is often grayish or bluish or marked with red, interesting on rock ledges where the soil is light and well drained, and wonderfully appropriate to old stone walls. The Wayside Gardens Co. photo

SPIRAEA
bridal-wreath   3 to 6 feet

SHRUB. This shrub, so much in vogue in nineteenth-century gardens, is very hardy

and can be depended upon to bloom year after year with minimum care. White flowers foam over the branches in spring. The foliage is attractive all summer, turns orange and red in autumn, and hangs on into winter with reddish stems. Earliest to bloom, in April, is S. *thunbergi* (illustrated), with tiny leaves and small flowers on arching branches. S. *prunifolia* in early May has long wands covered with button-sized very double flowers. S. *van houttei* blooms later with much larger clusters. Markedly different from the bridal-wreath types is S. *japonica* 'Anthony Waterer'. This is more stiff and erect, with flattish corymbs of rich pink flowers in late summer, and can be pruned to keep it low if desired. Spiraeas are excellent for accent, for backgrounds, for hedgerows. They need sun, but no special soil, and no pruning other than removing spent canes from the base. Walter Haring photo

STACHYS *lanata*
betony, lamb's-ears   8 to 12 inches

PERENNIAL. The rosettes of white-woolly leaves make this plant most effective as edging and in bedding but if so used the stalks of pale lavender rather inconspicuous flowers are best removed. It spreads rapidly, can become invasive, and must be divided every two or three years by removing the side crowns. Any soil in full sun seems to satisfy it, so long as there is ample water in dry weather. Walter Haring photo

STOKESIA *laevis*
Stoke's-aster   1 to 1½ feet

PERENNIAL. This very beautiful flower, somewhat like an exquisite China aster or a large centaurea, has never attained the popularity it deserves. Hardy and long-lived, it blooms, lavender, pinkish, or white, from mid-July to summer's end, and is excellent for cutting. Because the habit is sprawling and the foliage not profuse, it looks better in small groups among other plants, such as Shasta daisy, yellow snapdragon, and hypericum for complementary color or perhaps purple and lavender verbenas for harmony. Plant in mid-border in rich soil with full sun or light shade, and divide every third year. George W. Park Seed Co., Inc., photo

TRADESCANTIA *virginiana*
  spiderwort   12 to 20 inches

PERENNIAL. These are unpretentious
white, purple, or light lavender flowers in
few-flowered umbels above numerous grasslike leaves. The chief display is in late
June and early July but there are always
some flowers throughout the summer and
they have an appealing charm. However,
spiderwort tends to spread rapidly and
sprawls untidily and is probably best used
for naturalizing in the wild garden, in full
sun or semishade. Walter Haring photo

TRILLIUM *grandiflorum*
  wake-robin   1½ feet

PERENNIAL. Trilliums are members of the
lily family and native from Georgia to
Canada. The great white trillium is the
showiest. In the garden it will bloom in
spring with mertensia, brunnera, and di-
centra. Flowers are 3 inches across, slightly
cup-shaped, borne above a whorl of leaves
at the summit of the stem. Other species
have pink, purplish, or dark red flowers.
Plant in woodsy moist soil in partial shade.
Robert Miner photo

VIBURNUM   4 to 12 feet

SHRUB. The many American and introduced species of *Viburnum* are very dependable shrubs. The foliage is attractive, and usually turns scarlet, russet, or crimson in autumn. The late-spring flowers are conspicuous umbels of hundreds of white, in some varieties pink, florets, and are followed by colorful berries that last well into winter. Most viburnums are of open and spreading growth, ideal for backgrounds and along the edges of wide woodland paths. Popular now are *V. sieboldi,* growing in the author's garden (right), and *V. tomentosum,* single-file viburnum, whose horizontal branches produce tier upon tier of flat broad clusters of white flowers. The double form, *V. tomentosum sterile,* is the familiar snowball-bush. *V. carlcephalum* (below) is taller with larger, rounded heads of very fragrant flowers. The decorative *V. burkwoodi,* of lower stature, has blush-white flowers earlier than the other kinds and just as the leaves unfold. All viburnums like deep, moist, slightly acid soil and grow well in sun or light shade. *V. sieboldi,* Walter Haring photo; *V. carlcephalum,* The Wayside Gardens Co. photo

VINCA *rosea*
Madagascar periwinkle   3 to 18 inches

ANNUAL. This charming and accommodating plant is actually a short-lived perennial grown as an annual in the North. It is
one of the best bedding plants, being covered with flowers all summer—white, pink,
red, or lavender. Foliage is light green,
compact, and disease free. This vinca
withstands adverse conditions but responds
nobly to good soil and diligent watering.
There are some new dwarf varieties delightful for edging. 'Rose Carpet' grows to
6 inches, with deep pink flowers. 'Polka
Dot' is creeping, the flowers white with a
deep red eye—particularly good bordering
a bed of red geraniums or scarlet salvia.
Walter Haring photo

YUCCA *filamentosa*
Adam's-needle   4 to 6 feet

PERENNIAL. Yuccas are mostly desert
plants of the lily family, with evergreen
sword-shaped leaves in bold clusters and
tall imposing panicles of cream-white
flowers. This one species is native in the
Carolinas and will grow well in northern
gardens, flowering in July. It is particularly
striking against dark evergreens or at focal
points in the graden plan. It thrives best in
a sandy loam. The stiff leaves are greatly
prized for line in flower arrangements.
Walter Haring photo

ZINNIA 'Envy'   2½ to 3 feet

ANNUAL. A new color in zinnias, this
apple-green flower is multiple-rayed and
up to 3 inches across. Its cool green suggests many interesting combinations with
other flowers in the garden and in bouquets. In full sun the blossoms often take
on a more yellowish tinge, but where
somewhat shaded by foliage, they hold
their full green tone. Humus and superphosphate in the soil are recommended.
Walter Haring photo

3

Changing Concepts of Color

IN gardens, as in virtually all expressions of human activity, fashion plays a major, and yet often subtle, part. The modern gardener's palette can be as brilliant as the modern painter's. Plants can be selected that reflect the tonalities of one artist or another—the amazing dazzle of Van Gogh, the sombre richness of Rouault, the blended and luminous pastels of Monet, or the vibrant abstractions of Klee. Plant hybridizers have in the past decade provided us with a galaxy of new forms and new colors, pure tones that range from violent to misty, and with these the gardener can find material to carry out any creative impulse.

Today, since we entertain so much out of doors, colorful and unusual plantings at patio and terrace are stimulating and refreshing, especially when of striking color contrasts. You might use the large-flowered 'Carefree' geraniums, reds, pink, and orange together, or all the clashing strong colors of the plumed celosias. Our terrace in semishade terminates on one side in a planting of mixed begonias in a wide range of leaf colors from the almost black 'Bow Nigra' to the frosty white-and-green calla-lily begonia. Cane and cut-leaved types and tropical-looking Rexes provide a diversity of forms. At the other end of the terrace, still in semishade, a low stone wall reaches out and is topped with impatiens—white, pink, red, orange, and even the 'Garden Blues' in a deep magenta—discordant colors to be sure, but never failing to elicit the oh's and ah's of our guests.

Fine effects can be created by combining different varieties of one kind of plant. Coleus in deep velvety reds, fringed and variegated, interplanted with the gold-veined green ones, or broad bands of petunias in near-red, deep rose, and purple. Tulips, iris, daylilies, and other genera exhibiting a wide range of color, form, and height lend themselves to solid bed plantings. By selecting early, midseason, and late varieties, such displays can be sustained for many weeks. But the varieties of some plants, such as hostas, peonies, and many composites are all too similar to be used successfully alone. In any case, whatever combinations are chosen, the plants must be culturally content together. In the plant descriptions in this book I have limited companion plantings to those that require similar soil and growing conditions.

Where there is a considerable background of alleviating green, it is rarely possible for any combination of plants to appear too harsh, even when the inspiration is what we might call psychedelic. Examining the color pattern of a new silk fabric, I note contrasting diamonds of purple, brown, lavender, and orange. In the garden this could be emulated by using mixed zinnias, chrysanthemums, or dahlias, which certainly offer some violent hues. Another fabric is all swirls of magenta, cobalt blue, gold, and red! The once-despised magenta phlox with dark delphiniums, coreopsis, and red salvia could translate this effect—not in my garden to be sure but perhaps in yours, if such new concepts of color appeal to you.

In our long border plantings, I do use as centers of interest some of the strident colors: the red-plumed celosia 'Forest Fire', butterfly-weed (*Asclepias tuberosa*), cardinal-flower (*Lobelia cardinalis*), and some of the intense shades of phlox. However, I find these focal points are both accentuated and moderated by separating them with white or pale yellow flowers or by using gray-foliage plants such as artemisia or the annual *Centaurea gymnocarpa*. The deep bronzy-purple leaves of perilla make a strong contrast in almost any group of flowering plants.

Annuals can be grown in a separate cutting garden for bouquets or as replacements for the best-laid plan gone quite agley—the gladiolus that turns out to be violet instead of crimson and that you had set behind scarlet geraniums. Perhaps you will want to replace one or the other with silvery *Centaurea gymnocarpa* or *C.* 'Silver Queen' or with white snapdragons. Or you can let the accident remain, to shock the old-fashioned and bridge the generation gap for your young friends.

178

COMBINATIONS FOR EVERY SEASON

Whether you like your colors peaceful and harmonious or exciting and even discordant, you will find that nature and the extraordinary wealth of ornamental plants developed by hybridizers offer untold possibilities. Use your imagination—checking it only by the knowledge of what plants will really grow together in any specific conditions of soil, situation, climate, and moisture.

I personally prefer a sizable hardy border with big intergrading or contrasting patches of strong color but not in harsh juxtaposition. I like the feeling of nature—a garden that seems to blend with flowering shrubs, trees, and vines. Nevertheless, I have frequently been delighted by other styles of plantings. Some of these new color effects I might consider had I a different type of garden.

For most of the plants described and illustrated in this book, I have indicated some agreeable companions. Here are more color plans, taken—or adapted—from plantings that I have seen. They may suggest similar or variant combinations to suit your own taste and type of garden.

SPRING

Red, white, and blue for late April. A gay and unusual effect with the small scarlet *Tupila praestans* 'Fusilier', white hyacinths, and deep blue Siberian squills (*Scilla*). Or *Tulipa tarda* with *Arabis alpina* and orange-red pansies.

The floriferous mat-forming plants will now make sheets of color in the rock garden, and the white-flowered ones will enhance any color. *Arabis albida* and *Phlox subulata alba* come first, with the blazing scarlet *Tulipa eichleri*, violet-blue *Muscari armeniacum*, dark purple viola 'Jersey Gem', and the light but intense yellow *Viola tricolor alpina*. *Iberis sempervirens* follows, about the first of May, to provide masses of white background for dwarf iris and later tulips.

Early in spring the dwarf heath, *Erica tetralix mollis*, opens spikes of clear pink flowers, effective with rosy crimson *Armeria maritima laucheana* and the tiny *Mazus reptans,* whose flowers make carpets of solid mauve.

For late May, the yellow Korean *Rosa xanthina* and the shrublike *Rosa hugonis,* delightful with late iris.

Species of hardy pinks, pink and rose and white, above mounds of blue-green foliage are fine for broad edgings. *Dianthus plumarius* with fringed and frosty-looking flowers is lovely with the last of the scillas, *Scilla nonscripta rubra,* its 18-inch stems hung with rosy bells.

Azaleas for delicate or stirring effects: salmon-pink 'Mayflower' and salmon-shaded white 'Ruth May' with 'Delaware Valley White'; the burnt orange Exbury 'Gibraltar' with sulphur-yellow Ghent 'Narcissiflora'. Almost violent, and very telling: the dark-spotted salmon 'Guy Yerkes' with 'Purple Splendor', or bright crimson 'Hinodigiri' with clear red 'Stewartsonian', both with wine-red winter foliage.

For a pleasing association of rhododendrons: the small-leaved bright blue-violet 'Ramapo' and pure white 'Dora Amateis'; the large-leaved lavender dark-blotched 'Blue Peter', clear pink 'Scintillation', and white 'Boule de Neige'.

SPRING TO AUGUST

In the open shade of an apple tree, a series of pastels: pink bleeding hearts, lavender-blue Virginia bluebells, yellow doronicum, white *Trillium grandiflorum* all underplanted with self-sowing blue forget-me-nots. From June to August an edging of coralbells sends forth rose-colored sprays, and white feverfew runs through tall accents of golden daylilies and green cinnamon ferns.

Defining a shaded north-facing brick terrace a narrow bed of dwarf yew combined with hay-scented fern, a completely satisfying contrast of textures and very dark and very light greens, needing no flowers and a perfect transition from house to garden.

EARLY SUMMER

Centering a tile-floored patio, a raised bed of golden *Oenothera fruticosa,* a solid sheet of shining flowers almost all summer long. This planting would be enhanced by the deep orange, upright chalices of *Lilium croceum* in July and, from August to September, by the pendent trumpets of *L. henryi.*

180

Near a pond, Japanese iris in soft blue and blue-gray varieties rising above masses of astilbe with its imposing panicles of watermelon-pink, crushed-raspberry, and white flowers. The elegant foliage of the astilbe is as much a part of the effect as the flowers.

A long strip of pampas grass, 7 to 8 feet high, with thousands of feathery off-white plumes overhanging clumps of fiery red-hot-pokers.

Two glorious clematis adorning a garden fence. The white C. 'Henryi' and lavender-blue C. 'Ramona' are an excellent background for the perennial blue baptisia, white peonies, pink impatiens, and white-edged wax begonias.

Tall and dwarf campanulas for the end of June and through most of July, the upright ones in front of delphinium or with *Veronica spicata*, deep lavender alpine asters, and blue *Polemonium reptans*.

For a glowing red combination: *Lychnis chalcedonica*, with slashed scarlet petals behind the creeping fiery annual *Verbena hortensis* and the red geum 'Mrs. Bradshaw'—stunningly backed by the silver-green Waukegan juniper, *Juniperus horizontalis douglasi*.

For a gay combination: monarda 'Cambridge Red' with white phlox 'Miss Lingard' and blue balloon-flower (*Platycodon*).

MID- TO LATE SUMMER

In a city garden, a circle of mountain-ash trees in full orange fruit, underplanted with yellow and orange tuberous-rooted begonias.

In another landscape planting, orange-fruiting mountain-ash trees with purple-leaved plums behind them, hibiscus of a strong violet shade, and an underplanting of cerise zinnias. It sounds quite dreadful but actually is pleasing.

Eryngium amethystinum, 3 feet high, with its elaborately cut, broad white bracts and frosty-blue conelike flower-heads, behind scarlet salvia and orange African marigolds. This is one of the most astonishing and stunning juxtapositions—the icy-cool eryngium pacifying perfectly the discordant orange and red.

For mid-August to mid-September: orange and apricot cannas, with red-brown leaves, the tall *Lilium sulphureum*, and cosmos 'Fiesta' for lovely foliage and flame-colored stars. The late, light blue monkshood, *Aconitum fischeri*, and gladioli 'Bluebird' and 'Heavenly Blue'.

Hazy and dreamlike for September, *Hydrangea paniculata*, allowed to grow naturally above the lower shrub *Caryopteris mastacanthus,* a mist of violet flowers, and amongst them the tall lavender wands of the willow gentian, *G. asclepiadaea.*

The beautiful ground-cover *Plumbago larpentae,* with bright blue flowers in September, a brilliant edging for white and blue asters, yellow or pink or white bedding dahlias, perhaps interplanted with the large red-violet autumn crocus *Colchicum speciosum rubrum,* or with yellow stern-bergia.

A solid bed of the old favorite dahlia 'Bishop of Llandaff' with deep maroon foliage and crimson flowers, combined with the gold of the ever-blooming heliopsis 'Summer Sun' and blue *Salvia farinacea* for many weeks of exciting color.

EARLY TO LATE FALL

Tall pink-to-rose *Hibiscus syriacus,* lavender-blue chaste-tree, *Vitex macrophylla,* rose-pink *Tamarix* 'Summer Glow', with maroon *Rudbeckia* 'The Kings', underplanted with blue *Plumbago larpentae.*

FALL

Spectacular low-growing, hybrid goldenrods (solidago) planted with terra-cotta, garnet, mahogany, and a few white chrysanthemums with an edging of sempervivum 'Command Hay', its dense leaf rosettes of inter-grading olive-brown, sherry color, and red.

In October, the seldom seen low shrub, our native maple-leaved vibur-num (*Viburnum acerifolium*) has suede-textured foliage in tints of pink, old-rose, lavender, and clear yellow, all running together like the colors of a Chinese screen. White wild asters are beautiful with it and—if you can possibly grow it—the fringed gentian. All like a dampish and somewhat stony soil.

Golden sternbergia, in late September, like sunlight on the ground, backed by medium-height and then tall Michaelmas daisies in shades of lavender, pink, wine color, violet, and some whites. Fall asters grown this way in quantity are like a cloud of bonfire smoke, particularly lovely where yellow autumn leaves, as of silver maples, hang above them.

4

The Colors of the Year

Helen Van Pelt Wilson's garden. Walter Haring photo.

184

SPRING

And the Spring arose on the garden fair,
Like the Spirit of Love felt everywhere;
And each flower and herb on Earth's dark
　breast
Rose from the dreams of its wintry rest.

And the hyacinth purple, and white, and
　blue,
Which flung from its bells a sweet peal
　anew
Of music so delicate, soft, and intense,
It was felt like an odour within the sense.

Percy Bysshe Shelley

SPRING comes slowly, not overnight. To the casual observer the leaf buds on trees and shrubs open as if by magic, but the transformation is actually only part of a long development. In late February, flower buds of maples and elms are noticeably swelling, and the brown sheaths protecting the flowers of pussy willows have already split to display their hidden treasure of pinkish-gray catkins. Snowdrops expose their shyly drooping heads. Winter aconite unfurls its pale yellow buds. Even after a blanketing March snow has succumbed to a warmer bright day, these stalwarts still prevail to assure us of spring's advance. Soon, in the increasing strength of the sun, crocuses open their beautiful cups, basking in its glory until late afternoon. A walk around the garden shows that buds of many flowering shrubs and trees are eagerly waiting for just that right moment in April when they can confidently expand.

Spring colors are gently soft yet full of light. Pale greens, yellows, and whites are relieved and accented by the stronger tints of lavender and purple. Lawn grass is fresh and shimmery, quite unlike the deep green it will be in summer. Willows are pure gold against the sky. Leaves of flowering crabapples and cherries and some of the maples are rosy, tender, and satin soft. Early wild cherry and shadbush are fountains of white bloom. Magnolias hold out their rosy mauve and white chalices. Forsythia flashes through the landscape, and the first early tulips appear. May floods the world with the amazing foam of fruit trees in bloom. By the time azaleas begin to flower the transformation is complete.

Blues and lavenders also take their place in the procession. Scillas, grape-hyacinths, Virginia bluebells, forget-me-nots, and violets spread color over the ground.

Every year we stand in the midst of all this beauty. And every year the gardener is again inspired to emulate nature, to contribute his shade and make his own little world a part of the splendor.

185

Roses and delphinium in June. Franklin Photo Agency.

EARLY SUMMER

And what is so rare as a day in June?
Then, if ever, come perfect days;
Then Heaven tries the earth if it be in
tune,
And over it softly her warm ear lays:
Whether we look, or whether we listen,
We hear life murmur, or see it glisten.

Henry Wadsworth Longfellow

ENCHANTMENT surrounds us in early summer. The air is mild, the sky a soft blue; gardens are filled with perennial flowers. Louise Beebe Wilder once wrote: "What a chaos of beauty there is upon a June morning! Standing in the midst of the garden one experiences a sort of breathlessness of soul. June is so prodigal, so extravagant of all that makes the world beautiful, so kind to gardeners. We should be thankful for even one of the great flower families that grace this month . . . for the roses, the lupines, the peonies, the iris, but June comes to us with green apron recklessly overflowing, spreading her largess upon every hand until it is small wonder that we stand bewildered."

The dominant colors of early summer are pastel: light blue and lavender, pale pink and rose, and pale yellow, but enough of the deeper and richer hues are there to give substance, fullness, and even opulence to the garden. The background of shrubbery is dense and vivid green. The variety of flowers is extraordinary in form and texture—iris, delphinium, foxglove, astilbe, campanula, and many others. There is the magnificence of roses, peonies, and Oriental poppies and the delicacy of columbines and airy blue flax. Spires of subtly colored lupines and of white, lavender, and pale yellow foxgloves; stars and suns of lemon-lilies, pyrethrum, and doronicum. A thousand bells of campanulas swinging in the soft breeze or suspended in masses over a stone ledge. Here and there the pure forms of madonna and regal lilies.

In June the frivolities of spring are past, it is the season of serious beginnings. Young creatures are becoming wise under the watchful eyes of their parents. The world is full of purpose and promise. Orioles, cardinals, and thrushes celebrate the joy of being alive. And in the midst of our garden work we suddenly find ourself forsaking the spade or the trowel, to wonder and celebrate, too.

Riot of color in a Vermont garden. Franklin Photo Agency.

MIDSUMMER

There are striped zinnias that bees fly far
   to visit;
And sweet peas . . . sunflowers and holly-
   hocks
And pink or yellow four o'clocks.
Here are humming birds come to seek the
Tall delphinium.

Louise Driscoll

IN mid- to late summer the garden picture has changed. The strong, bright colors of the advancing season thrill and excite us. Phlox in all its vivid hues of pink, rose, salmon, and coral contrasts with the purity of Shasta daisy and the yellows of the midsummer perennials: achillea, heliopsis, daylilies. Orange butterfly-weed, golden helenium, and scarlet bee-balm occupy commanding places. The paint-box hues of the annuals—petunias, zinnias, marigolds, snapdragons, and asters—splash vibrant color on beds and borders, the brightness accentuated by the deep green of shrubs and evergreen backgrounds. Late hardy lilies are exotic and sumptuous. Morning glories riot over porches, fences, and arbors. Gladiolus lift long spears of rich colors. Early dahlias are big pompons or rosettes or wide-rayed suns. After a summer shower the air is sparkling and the freshly washed greens and grays of foliage plants stand out sharply against all these deep and dramatic colors of flowers.

Blues and lavenders of veronica, balloon-flower, globe-thistle, monkshood, and salvia provide oases of coolness. Or, of course, one may have a mid-July and August garden largely composed of blue and lavender flowers, for there are many, including the shrubs buddleia, hydrangea, vitex, and Rose-of-Sharon 'Bluebird'. A generous use of white will bring life to the blues and still keep the "cool." White phlox, white physostegia, *Veronica* 'Icicle', *Liatris* 'White Spire', and *Lilium longifolium formosum* are reliable hardy plants. The white varieties of annuals are legion.

Midsummer is the season of fulfillment, the time when many perennials and most annuals reach their climax in a dazzling display. The gardener may rest a bit to see what his hand hath wrought.

Chrysanthemums in October. Paul E. Genereux photo.

AUTUMN

Season of mists and mellow fruitfulness,
Close bosom-friend of the maturing sun;
Conspiring with him how to load and bless
With fruit the vines that round the thatch-
eaves run;
To bend with apples the moss'd cottage-
trees,
And fill all fruit with ripeness to the core;
To swell the gourd, and plump the hazel
shells
With a sweet kernel; to set budding more,
And still more, later flowers for the bees,
Until they think warm days will never
cease,
For Summer has o'er-brimmed their clammy
cells.

John Keats

IN America, the colors of autumn are so brilliant that even on a gray day the world seems touched with light. Skies are usually a clear, deep blue, the air like mountain water. Blue jays scream their warnings; squirrels, chipmunks, and field mice work overtime. All of nature is hastening to flower and fruit and seed before the inevitable frost.

In yards and gardens and country roadsides color everywhere catches our eye. Marigolds, zinnias, asters, and scarlet sage take on an even more intense hue. Roses, deepening in color in response to cooler weather, continue their display until heavy frost coats each bud with silvery rime. Chrysanthemums, Michaelmas daisies, and dahlias bloom with reckless abandon. Sugar maples, red maples, sumac, some oaks are seemingly set on fire. Fruits of viburnums, of flowering crabapples and of mountain-ash hang like luminous jewels. The orange and gold of pumpkin and bittersweet, the fading purple of ripened grapes; the scarlet of woodbine and burning-bush rival the sunsets.

Crickets and katydids utter what man cannot say. A curious fragrance pervades the air . . . of goldenrod, wild asters, wood smoke, fallen apples. It is the season of harvest and accomplishment, bringing with it a great sense of peace. The garden dies down to wait for the cycle of the year to begin again in spring.

191

Red-berried viburnum at Longwood Gardens. Walter Hampfler photo.

192

WINTER

I, singulary moved
To love the lovely that are not beloved,
Of all Seasons most
Love Winter . . .

Nor is in field or garden anything
But, duly look'd into, contains serene
The substance of things hoped for, in the
  Spring
And evidence of Summer not yet seen.

Coventry Patmore

THE winter garden is not without touches of color. There can be more color if you study the possibilities of trees and shrubs which are hardy in your locality and plant some of them in your garden. It is a joy to see from inside the house the varied colors of evergreens, of bark, and of berries. Pine and spruce are blue-green, andromeda almost apple-green, euonymus and abelia warm reddish-bronze. From my dining room window in January I see many colors: the purple of Bar Harbor juniper in its winter dress, the red-gold of the twigs of *Spiraea thunbergi,* the red and brown branches of the crabapple trees. The scarlet berries of *Viburnum theiferum, V. trilobum,* and *V. opulus* hang on all winter and provide food for cedar waxwings and robins. Near them a golden weeping willow extends its long yellow wands. Sometimes winter colors become brilliant against new-fallen snow. In some weather the colors are muted and subtle. At twilight the naked stems of the sugar maple turn to silver against the gold and rose of the sunset. Such a glow is cast over the garden that many shrubs appear to be deep violet or purple. Pines, spruces, and hemlocks darken and are filled with mysterious shadows.

In sheltered spots of our meadow, small patches of green grass contrast vividly with the twigs of red osier dogwood and the tan and rose twigs of wild blueberry. Oak leaves of tarnished gold still cling to their perilous perches despite winter winds. Dark red berries of *Rosa multiflora* and *Rosa rugosa* gleam in the sunlight.

With proper selection there need be few entirely brown or gray spots in the winter garden. Summer color is easily accomplished, but winter color involves a real knowledge of plants and how to place them strategically. Beyond that, Winter is an unpredictable impresario: If you provide the setting, he can change it overnight into fairyland.

193

5

Useful Lists

FRAGRANT FLOWERS

THIS list is restricted to those flowers that have a powerful scent, "free" on the air and pervasive for some distance in the garden.

Azalea (*Rhododendron*) *arborescens, atlanticum, roseum, viscosum,* and a
   few hybrids
Buddleia, especially 'Charming', 'Ile de France', 'White Profusion'
Cheiranthus
Chionanthus
Clematis montana, paniculata
Clethra
Convallaria
Daphne cneorum
Datura
Heliotropium arborescens
Hemerocallis citrina, flava, and some hybrids, as 'Hyperion' and 'Midwest
   Majesty'
Hesperis
Hyacinthus

Iris, some tall bearded, as *pallida dalmatica*, and some hybrids, as 'Blue
  Sapphire' and 'Great Lakes'
Ismene calathina
Lathyrus odoratus
Lavandula
Lilium auratum, candidum, regale, sargentianum, and 'Pink Glory' strain
Lobularia maritima
Lonicera japonica halliana
Magnolia
Malus angustifolia, baccata, ionensis plena, and some hybrids, as 'Hopa'
  and 'Kaido'
Mathiola incana
Narcissus
Nicotiana
Paeonia albiflora
Philadelphus lemoinei
Phlox decussata
Prunus amygdalus, serrulata, subhirtella, triloba, and 'Toka'
Reseda odorata
Rosa. Some floribundas, hybrid teas, and other modern roses have little or
  no scent. Many, however, are strongly fragrant, among them 'Chrysler
  Imperial', 'Crimson Glory', 'The Doctor', 'Fashion', 'Ma Perkins', 'Mc-
  Gredy's Ivory', and 'Orange Sensation'. The hybrid perpetual 'Mrs. John
  Laing' and the rugosa 'Blanc Double de Coubert' are outstandingly
  fragrant. Some species known for this attribute are *R. damascena, gal-
  lica, multiflora, rubiginosa* (sweet brier), and *wichuraiana.*
Syringa vulgaris and most hybrids
Valeriana officinalis
Viburnum carlesii
Wisteria

COLORS BY THE SCORE

YELLOW TO ORANGE

Alyssum	Chrysanthemum	Evening-primrose	Laburnum
Blanket-flower	Crown Imperial	Forsythia	Marigold
Butterfly-weed	Daffodil	Gloriosa Daisy	Primrose
Calendula	Daylily	Helen's-flower	St. John's-wort
California Poppy	Doronicum	Iris	Tulip

PINK TO ROSE

Azalea	Columbine	Michaelmas Daisy	Rhododendron
Beauty-bush	Creeping Phlox	Painted Daisy	Salvia 'Rose Glow'
Bleeding-heart	False-dragonhead	Peony	Snapdragon
Canterbury Bell	Hollyhock	Petunia	Tulip
Chrysanthemum	Loosestrife	Pinks	Weigela

RED

Anemone	Dahlia	Peony	Sprekelia
Beebalm	Daylily	Phlox	Sweet-William
Cockscomb	Firethorn	Rose	Red-twig Dogwood
Chrysanthemum	Maltese Cross	Salvia	Tulip
Crabapple 'Red Jade'	Oriental Poppy	Sedum	Zinnia

BLUE TO PURPLE

Ageratum	Flax	Michaelmas Daisy	Summer Forget-me-not
Blue-mist-flower	Grape-hyacinth	Plumbago	
China Aster	Iris	Rose of Sharon	Stoke's-aster
Cornflower	Lobelia	Salvia 'Blue Bedder'	Tulip
Delphinium	Lupine	Squill	Virginia Bluebells
			Veronica

WHITE AND GREEN

African Daisy	Chrysanthemum	Lily-of-the-valley	Peony
Angel's-trumpet	Feverfew	Madonna Lily	Shasta Daisy
Arabis	Fringetree	Nicotiana	Silver-bell-tree
Baby's-breath	Gas-plant	Phlox	Snapdragon
Candytuft	Iris	Oriental Poppy	Star Magnolia

EFFECTIVE COMBINATIONS

Spring

YELLOW TO ORANGE

Bronze tulips, wallflowers, and flax.
Chrysogonum, white trillium, and wood ferns.
Cornelian-cherry underplanted with pale yellow daffodils.
Crown imperial, yellow alyssum, and *Tulipa greigii* 'Cape Cod'.
Daffodils, arabis, and lavender creeping phlox.
Forsythia, blue chionodoxa, and yellow and white crocus.
Lavender *Iris cristata* with yellow alyssum, and spring forget-me-nots.
Leopard's-bane, daffodils, and scarlet and yellow-orange tulips.
Pale yellow and lavender tulips, orange wallflowers, and hardy candytuft.
Primroses, forget-me-nots, ferns, and Virginia bluebells.
Siberian wallflowers, blue flax, white columbine, and early yellow daylilies.
Tulipa tarda, rockcress, and blue lungwort.
Yellow tulips, hardy candytuft, and blue *Scilla sibirica.*

PINK TO ROSE

Pink azalea, with blue and white *Scilla campanulata.*
Pink and lilac tulips, white poet's narcissus, and leopard's-bane.
Bleeding-heart, Virginia bluebells, and ferns.
Candystick tulips with purple and white pansies.
Creeping phlox, arabis, and dark blue pansies.
Daphne with *Scilla sibirica.*
Japanese cherry, pale yellow daffodils, and blue *Iris pumila.*
Pink azalea with purple Darwin tulips.
Pink flowering-almond, white and pale yellow tulips, and grape-hyacinths.
Pink crabapple, yellow and white tulips, and hardy candytuft.
Pink flowering-quince underplanted with rockcress, yellow alyssum, and
grape-hyacinths.

RED

Red and white anemones with tulip 'De Wet'.
Red and white tulips, candytuft, Virginia bluebells, and pale yellow
  alyssum.
Red Emperor tulips with pale yellow and gold daffodils.
Scarlet and white tulips, pale blue pansies, and white candytuft.
Sprekelia, white candytuft, and yellow alyssum.
Tulipa praestans, Virginia bluebells, and white hyacinths.

BLUE TO PURPLE

Sky-blue brunnera, white candytuft, and yellow alyssum.
Blue lungwort, yellow *Tulipa tarda,* and pink hyacinths.
Chionodoxa, daffodils, and waterlily tulips.
Early purple iris with leopard's-bane.
Forget-me-nots, yellow alyssum, purple pansies, and yellow and white
  tulips.
Grape-hyacinths, white peony-flowered tulips, and narcissus 'Cheerfulness'.
Iris pumila and candytuft.
Iris reticulata, pink and white hyacinths, and Lenten-roses.
Wild sweet-William, white candytuft, and yellow primroses.
Lavender and mauve tulips with pale yellow pansies and white hardy
  candytuft.
Wisteria with pink, white, and purple tulips and wild sweet-William.

WHITE

Christmas- or Lenten-roses, white *Scilla sibirica,* and blue *Iris reticulata.*
Daffodil 'Cheerfulness', bleeding-heart, forget-me-nots, and mauve violas.
Dogwood, pink azalea, and blue and white *Scilla campanulata.*
Peony-flowered tulips and everblooming bleeding-heart.
Narcissua poeticus, bleeding-heart, and white creeping phlox.
Snowdrops with lavender and yellow crocus.
Star magnolia underplanted with *Scilla sibirica* and grape-hyacinths.
White pansies, lilac and yellow tulips, and pasque-flowers.
White lily-flowered tulips with Virginia bluebells.

Early Summer

YELLOW TO ORANGE

Aquilegia chrysantha and *Veronica incana.*
Coreopsis, lavender penstemon, and foxglove.
Yellow foxglove, pink coralbells, white feverfew, and evening-primrose.
Gaillardia, blue peach-leaved bellflowers, and daylilies.
Orange geum, yellow iris, and golden centaurea.
Yellow iris, gas-plant, and buttercup-bush.
Pale yellow iris, blue lupine, and white columbine.
Lily 'Enchantment', delphinium 'Connecticut Yankee', and gaillardia.
Fernleaf yarrow, blue delphinium, globe-thistle, and butterfly-weed.

PINK TO ROSE

Canterbury bells with mauve and pink iris.
Coralbells, foxglove, white lilies, and blue lupine.
Japanese peonies, heliopsis 'Summer Sun', and Siberian iris.
Painted daisy, Canterbury bells, and white foxglove.
Pink and white peonies with white and blue peach-leaved bellflowers.
Pink and blush dianthus, catmint, and thrift.
Sweet-William 'Newport Pink', catmint, and phlox 'Miss Lingard'.

RED

Oriental poppies, catmint, and artemisia.
Red peonies, pale yellow lupine, and blue tradescantia.
Maltese cross, white foxglove, and dark red sweet-William.

BLUE TO PURPLE

Blue and white delphinium, lemon-yellow evening-primrose, and yellow and rose columbine.
Flax, coreopsis, lavender iris, white columbine, and lemon daylilies.

Mauve and lavender iris, yellow columbine, blue flax, and coralbells.
Lavender iris, white and pink Oriental poppies, and catmint.
Blue, rose, and pink lupine with yellow to white iris.
Purple, mauve, and pink Japanese iris with white and rose astilbe.
Salvia 'Oestfriesland', with rose peonies, and pale yellow yarrow 'Moon-shine'.
Summer forget-me-nots, lavender, pink or white Oriental poppies, and coralbells.

WHITE AND GREEN

White columbine, summer forget-me-nots, pink lupine, and white veronica.
Madonna lilies, blue veronica, and pink fleabane.
White Oriental poppies, pale blue iris, and deep rose peonies.
White peach-leaved bellflowers, coralbells, and summer forget-me-nots.
Regal lilies, balloon-flowers, and pale yellow daylilies.

Midsummer

YELLOW TO ORANGE

Achillea 'Coronation Gold', red monarda, and veronica 'Icicle'.
Calendula, lavender stokesia, ageratum, blue cornflower, and white and yellow snapdragons.
California poppies and kingfisher daisies.
Celosia 'Golden Fleece', mauve China asters, and pale yellow zinnias.
Gloriosa daisy 'Pinwheel', red daylilies, evening-primrose, and delphinium.
Daylilies, coralbells, Madonna lilies.
Gaillardia, regal lilies, balloon-flowers, and *Oenothera missouriensis*.
Heliopsis 'Goldsturm', pale yellow daylilies, and dark blue delphinium.
Lemon daylilies, phlox 'Miss Lingard', and blue-gray *Veronica incana*.
Mid-Century or Fiesta hybrid lilies, Shasta daisies, pale yellow daylilies, and blue *Veronica spicata*.
Pale yellow marigolds and basil 'Dark Opal'.
Yellow marguerites, blue veronica, and white feverfew.
Zinnia 'Bonanza', gloriosa daisies, yellow snapdragons, and marigold 'Primrose'.

PINK TO ROSE

Pink to lavender bedding dahlias edged with alyssum 'Rosie O'Day'.

Pink, rose, lavender, and white impatiens, with coleus and pink and white wax begonias.

Jewels of Opar edged with ageratum.

Lythrum 'Morden's Gleam', white phlox, blue veronica, and delphinium 'Connecticut Yankee'.

Phlox drummondi with anchusa 'Blue Bird'.

Pink petunias edged with lobelia 'Crystal Palace'.

Pink to rose Shirley poppies and annual white baby's-breath.

Pink zinnias with white verbena, edged with dwarf ageratum.

Rose zinnias with cineraria 'Frosty'.

Rosy milfoil, false-dragonhead, hardy pinks, and baby's-breath.

Rudbeckia 'Bright Star', regal lilies, and yarrow 'Coronation Gold'.

Salvia 'Rose Glow' and pale yellow Mexican tulip-poppy.

Pink, salmon, rose, carmine, and white summer phlox, artemisia 'Silver King', delphinium 'Connecticut Yankee', and white China asters.

Pink and white snapdragons with Chinese forget-me-nots.

Tuberous-rooted begonias, ferns, and hosta.

RED

Maltese cross, blue balloon-flowers, and white veronica.

Cannas edged with marigold 'Yellow Nugget'.

Celosia 'Fiery Feather', pink petunias, and lobelia 'Blue Stone'.

Geraniums with dusty miller centaurea.

Red and yellow dwarf dahlias, verbena 'Amethyst', and feverfew.

Shirley poppies and Chinese forget-me-nots or anchusa 'Blue Bird'.

Red and white zinnias and salvia 'Blue Bedder', edged with sweet alyssum.

Scarlet sage, blue ageratum, and white alyssum.

Scarlet sweet-William with purple and white petunias.

BLUE TO PURPLE

Anchusa 'Blue Bird', celosia 'Fiery Feather', and vinca 'Little Bright Eye'.

Blue delphinium with regal or Madonna lilies.

Stokesia, Shasta daisies, St. John's-wort, and purple verbena.

Blue-lace-flower, yellow marguerites, yellow or white snapdragons, baby's-breath, and sea-lavender.

Gayfeather with pink and white summer phlox.

Blue, white, and pink China asters, white snapdragons, and salvia 'Blue Bedder'.

Blue petunias with white and pink alyssum.

Cornflower, yellow marigolds, and pink and white zinnias.

Globe-thistle with pink and white gladiolus.

Larkspur and pale yellow petunias.

Lavender, white, and yellow zinnias edged with white petunias.

WHITE

Angel's-trumpet, cleome 'Pink Queen', Chinese forget-me-nots, pink snapdragons, and white petunias.

Orange impatiens with white wax begonias.

White petunias, bells of Ireland, nicotiana 'Lime Sherbet', zinnia 'Envy', and pale yellow marigolds.

Madonna lilies and pink baby's-breath.

Phlox 'Miss Lingard', monarda 'Cambridge Red', and delphinium 'Connecticut Yankee'.

White stock, mauve heliotrope, and pink cosmos.

White petunias and pink geraniums.

White phlox, pink lythrum, and pale yellow daylilies.

White, yellow, and carmine snapdragons with blue, white, and rose petunias.

White phlox, gloriosa daisies, Chinese forget-me-nots, and blue veronica.

Late Summer and Autumn

YELLOW TO ORANGE

Kniphofia, lavender China asters, and ageratum.

Helenium 'Autumnale', kniphofia, and lavender Michaelmas daisies.

Bronze chrysanthemums, salvia 'Blue Bedder', and yellow dahlias.

Daylilies, kniphofia, and dwarf marigolds, edged with blue ageratum.

Solidago 'Golden Mosa' with Michaelmas daisies 'Blue Radiance' or 'Harrington's Pink'.

Imperial Goldband lilies with celosia 'Golden Triumph' and white zinnias.

Marigolds, salvia 'Blue Bedder', and dwarf lavender chrysanthemums.

PINK TO ROSE

Hardy ageratum with pink, white, and rose chrysanthemums.
Pink Michaelmas daisies and plumbago.
Deep pink dahlias with white and mauve Michaelmas daisies.
Salvia azurea, Lilium speciosum, and Michaelmas daisy 'Harrington's Pink'.

RED

Scarlet, crimson, and white dahlias, faced with medium-height red and white cosmos.
Tithonia, cockscomb, and artemisia 'Silver King'.
Red *Anemone japonica* with red and white snapdragon.
Wine-red chrysanthemums, snow-on-the-mountain, and late sweet-alyssum.
Firethorn against a wall or fence, with abelia below, and orange chrysanthemums in front.
Scarlet sage, French marigolds, and white sea-lavender.
Scarlet sage, hardy ageratum, and late red-and-white petunias.
Rose-red rudbeckia 'The King', white gayfeather, and orange kniphofia.

BLUE TO PURPLE

Lavender and white chrysanthemums, mauve Michaelmas daisies, and late lily 'Formosa'.
Blue lobelia, cardinal-flower, and early white chrysanthemums.
Michaelmas daisies with Aurelian hybrid lilies.
Dark blue Michaelmas daisies with lily 'Silver Imperial', pink phlox, and dwarf white chrysanthemum 'Ostosa'.

WHITE

White and pink dahlias with mauve Michaelmas daisies.
Lily 'Silver Imperial', pink phlox, and dwarf white chrysanthemums.
Lily 'Formosa' and pink Michaelmas daisies.
White Japanese anemones and hardy ageratum.

6

A Quick-Reference Chart

If a plant blooms in more than one color, the text *description* will be found in the color group indicated by a boldface **X**. Other colors in which the flower is available are noted by a lightface X. Plants grown primarily or partly for their colorful or whitish leaves are designated by XL, and those which have conspicuous fruits by XF. Reference to a green flower is indicated by G.

A QUICK-REFERENCE CHART
See preceding page for key

PLANT	Height in feet	Season of bloom	Yellow to Orange (Y)	Pink to Rose (P)	Red (R)	Blue to Purple (B)	White and Green (W)
ABELIA GRANDIFLORA .... bush-arbutus	3–6	June to frost		X			
ABELIOPHYLLUM DISTICHUM .... white-forsythia	3½–5	Early spring					X
ACIDANTHERA BICOLOR .... peacock-orchid	2–3	Late summer					X
ACHILLEA-FILIPENDULINA .... fernleaf yarrow	3–4	Midsummer	X				
ACHILLEA MILLEFOLIUM .... rosy milfoil	2–3	Midsummer		X			
AETHIONEMA GRANDIFLORUM .... Persian stonecress	under 1	Spring		X			
AGERATUM COELESTINUM .... floss-flower	under 1	July to frost				X	X
AJUGA GENEVENSIS .... bugle-plant	½	Late spring		X		X	X
ALLIUM (various) .... ornamental onion	under 1 to 5	June– July	X	X		X	X
ALSTROEMERIA .... Peruvian-lily	2–4	Summer	X	X			
ALTHAEA ROSEA .... hollyhock	6–8	Early summer	X	X	X		X
ALYSSUM SAXATILE .... basket-of-gold	1–1½	Spring	X				
AMARANTHUS CAUDATUS .... Joseph's-coat, love-lies-bleeding	3–5	Summer	X	X			G
AMELANCHIER ASIATICA .... Juneberry, shadbush	10	Spring					X
ANCHUSA CAPENSIS .... summer forget-me-not	1½	Midsummer				X	

PLANT	Height in feet	Season of bloom	Y	P	R	B	W
ANDROMEDA CATESBAEI drooping leucothoe	2–3	Early spring					X
ANEMONE JAPONICA windflower	2–3	Fall		X	X		X
ANEMONE PULSATILLA pasque-flower	under 1	Spring				X	
ANEMONE BLANDA, CORONARIA windflower	under 1			X		X	X
ANTHEMIS TINCTORIA camomile, marguerite	2–3	Summer	X				
ANTIRRHINUM MAJUS snapdragon	1–3	July to frost	X	X	X		X
AQUILEGIA (various) columbine	1½–2	May–June	X	X		X	X
AQUILEGIA FLABELLATA NANA dwarf Japanese columbine	1	Spring					X
ARABIS ALBIDA rockcress	½	Early spring					X
ARCTOTIS GRANDIS blue-eyed daisy	1–2	Summer	X	X	X		X
ARGEMONE GRANDIFLORA prickly-poppy	2½–3	July to frost	X			X	X
ARMERIA MARITIMA thrift or sea-pink	1	Late spring		X			
ARONIA ARBUTIFOLIA chokeberry	5–6	May			XF		X
ARTEMISIA (various) wormwood, southernwood	1½–3	(leaves)					XL
ASCLEPIAS TUBEROSA butterfly-weed	2	Summer	X				
ASTER (hybrids) Michaelmas daisy	1½–4	Late summer, autumn		X		X	X
ASTILBE JAPONICA false-spirea	1½–2	June		X	X		X
AZALEA (various)	1–5	Spring	X	X		X	X

PLANT	Height in feet	Season of bloom	Y	P	R	B	W
BEGONIA SEMPERFLORENS wax begonia	1	Summer		X	X		X
BEGONIA TUBERHYBRIDA tuberous rooted	1½–2	Summer	X	X	X	X	X
BELLIS PERENNIS English daisy	½	Spring		X	X		X
BERGENIA CORDIFOLIA saxifrage	1	Spring		X			X
BRACHYCOME IBERIDIFOLIA Swan-River daisy	1	July–Aug.		X		X	X
BROWALLIA ELATA amythyst-flower	1–1½	Summer				X	X
BRUNNERA MACROPHYLLA large-leaved forget-me-not	1	May				X	
CALADIUM BICOLOR	1–2	(leaves)		XL			XL
CALENDULA OFFICINALIS pot-marigold	1½	July to frost	X				X
CALLIOPSIS TINCTORIA	under 1–1½	Summer	X	X			
CALLISTEPHUS CHINENSIS China aster	1–3	Summer	X	X		X	X
CALLUNA VULGARIS heather	1–1½	Late winter		X		X	X
CALTHA PALUSTRIS marsh-marigold	1	April	X				
CAMASSIA quamash	1½–3	May–June				X	
CAMELLIA JAPONICA	5–20	Fall–spring		X	X		X
CAMELLIA SASANQUA	1	Winter–spring		X			X
CAMPANULA CARPATICA bellflower	under 1	Summer				X	
CAMPANULA MEDIUM Canterbury-bells	3	June–July		X		X	X
CAMPANULA PERSICIFOLIA peach-leaved bellflower	2½–3	June				X	X

208

PLANT	Height in feet	Season of bloom	Y	P	R	B	W
CAMPSIS RADICANS .... trumpet-vine	25	Late summer	X				
CANNA 	1½–5	Summer	X	X			X
CARYOPTERIS CLANDONENSIS .... blue-mist-flower, hardy blue-spirea	2½–3	Aug. to frost				X	
CELOSIA ARGENTEA .... cockscomb	1–4	Aug. to frost	X	X	X	X	
CENTAUREA CYANUS .... bachelor's-button, cornflower	1½–3	Summer	X	X		X	X
CENTAUREA GYMNOCARPA .... dusty miller	1–1½	(leaves)	X				XF
CENTAUREA MACROCEPHALA .... golden centaurea	3	July	X				
CERASTOSTIGMA LARPENTIAE .... plumbago	under 1	Aug.– Sept.				X	
CERCIS CANADENSIS .... redbud, Judas-tree	6–20	Early spring		X			
CHAENOMELES JAPONICA .... flowering-quince	2–6	Early spring		X	X		X
CHEIRANTHUS ALLIONI .... wallflower	1–2	Spring	X				
CHIONANTHUS VIRGINICA .... fringetree, old-man's-beard	10–20	Early June					X
CHIONODOXA LUCILIAE .... glory-of-the-snow	under 1	Early spring				X	
CHRYSANTHEMUM COCCINEUM ...... painted daisy, pyrethrum	1½–2½	May– June		X			
CHRYSANTHEMUM HORTORUM .... garden chrysanthemum	1–4	Aug.– Nov.	X	X			X
CHRYSANTHEMUM MAXIMUM .... Shasta daisy	2–3	July– Sept.					X
CHRYSANTHEMUM CARINATUM ...... summer chrysanthemum	1½	Late summer	X	X		X	X
CHRYSOGONUM VIRGINIANUM 	1	May to July	X				

209

PLANT	Height in feet	Season of bloom	Y	P	R	B	W
CINERARIA MARITIMA dusty miller	1	(leaves)					XL
CLEMATIS (various)	4–12	Summer	X	X		X	X
CLEOME SPINOSA spider-flower	2–5	Summer		X			X
CLETHRA ALNIFOLIA sweet pepperbush	3–6	July– Aug.		X			X
COLCHICUM AUTUMNALE meadow-saffron	under 1	Fall		X		X	X
COLEUS BLUMEI	1–3	(leaves)		XL	XL		XL
CONVALLARIA MAJALIS lily-of-the-valley	under 1	Spring					X
COREOPSIS GRANDIFLORA tickseed	2–3	June– Sept.	X				
CORNUS FLORIDA dogwood	20	May– June			XF		X
CORNUS KOUSA Korean dogwood	20	June			XF		X
CORNUS MAS Cornelian-cherry	10	Early spring	X		XF		
COSMOS BIPINNATUS	2½–6	Summer	X	X		X	X
COTONEASTER (various)	2–4	Spring			XF		
CRATAEGUS (various) hawthorn	10–20	Spring		X	XF		X
CROCUS (various)	under ½	Early spring	X			X	X
CYCLAMEN (various)	under 1	Aug.– Sept.		X			X
CYNOGLOSSUM AMABILE Chinese forget-me-not	1½–2	July to frost				X	X
CYTISUS PRAECOX Warminster broom	4–5	May	X				
DAHLIA (various)	1–5	Summer– fall	X	X		X	X
DAPHNE CNEORUM garland-flower	1	Spring– autumn		X			

PLANT	Height in feet	Season of bloom	Y	P	R	B	W
DATURA STRAMONIUM angel's-trumpet, moonflower	3–5	Summer				X	X
DELPHINIUM AJACIS annual larkspur	1–4	June–July		X		X	X
DELPHINIUM (hybrids) perennial larkspur	2½–6	June–July		X		X	X
DIANTHUS BARBATUS sweet-William	1–1½	June		X	X		X
DIANTHUS CHINENSIS annual pinks	1	June to frost		X	X		X
DIANTHUS (various) garden pinks	½–1	Spring–summer		X	X		X
DICENTRA EXIMIA	1–1½	Spring to frost		X			
DICENTRA SPECTABILIS bleeding-heart	2–2½	Spring		X			
DICTAMNUS FRAXINELLA gas-plant	2–3	May		X			X
DIDISCUS CAERULEA blue-lace-flower	1½–2	July to frost				X	
DIGITALIS PURPUREA foxglove	3	June	X	X		X	X
DIGITALIS AMBIQUA foxglove	3	June	X				
DIMORPHOTHECA (hybrids) star-of-the-veldt	1–1½	Summer	X	X			X
DORONICUM CLUSI leopard's-bane	1½–3	Early spring	X				
EMILIA SAGITTATA tassel-flower	1½	Summer	X		X		
ERANTHIS HYEMALIS winter-aconite	under 1	Feb.–Mar.	X				
EREMURUS (various) foxtail-lily	3–6	June–July	X	X		X	X
ERICA (various) heath	½–2	Feb.–Apr.		X			

211

PLANT	Height in feet	Season of bloom	Y	P	R	B	V
ERIGERON KARVINSKIANUS .... fleabane	2–2½	Summer	X	X		X	
ERYNGIUM AMETHYSTINUM .... sea-holly	2½–3	July– Aug.				X	
ERYTHRONIUM (various) .... trout-lily, dogtooth-violet	under 1	Early spring	X	X			X
ESCHSCHOLTZIA CALIFORNICA .... California poppy	1–1½	July to frost	X	X			X
EUONYMUS ALATUS COMPACTUS ...... dwarf flame-bush, burning-bush	4–6				XLF		
EUONYMUS RADICANS VEGETUS ...... winter-creeper	30				XF		
EUPATORIUM COELESTINUM .... hardy ageratum, mist-flower	3–4	Aug.– Sept.				X	X
EUTOCA CAMPANULARIA .... bee's-friend, California bluebell	1	Mid- summer				X	
EUPHORBIA MARGINATA .... snow-on-the-mountain	2–3	(leaves)					X
EXOCHORDA (various) .... pearl-bush	4–6	Apr.– May					X
FORSYTHIA (various) .... goldenbells	4–8	Early spring	X				
FRITILLARIA IMPERIALIS .... crown imperial	1½–3	Apr.– May	X				X
FRITILLARIA MELEAGRIS .... guinea-hen-flower	1–1½	Apr.– May				X	X
GAILLARDIA (hybrids) .... blanket-flower	1–2½	June– Sept.	X		X		
GALANTHUS NIVALIS .... snowdrop	under 1	Early spring					X
GAZANIA (hybrids) .... African daisy	1–1½	Summer	X	X			X
GERANIUM (various) .... cranesbill	1–1½	Spring or summer		X		X	X
GERBERIA JAMESONI .... Transvaal daisy	1½	Summer	X	X	X		

PLANT	Height in feet	Season of bloom	Y	P	R	B	W
GEUM AURANTIACUM avens	1–1½	May– June	X	X	X		
GLADIOLUS (various)	1½–5	Summer	X	X	X	X	X
GLORIOSA ROTHSCHILDIANA gloriosa-lily	2–3	Late summer	X		X		
GODETIA GRANDIFLORA satin-flower	1–1½	Summer		X		X	X
GOMPHRENA GLOBOSA globe-amaranth	2	Mid- summer	X		X	X	X
GYPSOPHILA PANICULATA hardy baby's-breath	2–4	June– July		X			X
GYPSOPHILA ELEGANS baby's-breath	1–1½	June		X			X
GYPSOPHILA REPENS	1	June– July		X			X
HALESIA CAROLINA silver-bell-tree	15	May					X
HELENIUM (hybrids) Helen's-flower	2½–4	Aug.– Sept.	X		X		
HELIANTHUS (hybrids) sunflower	1½–6	Summer	X				X
HELICHRYSUM BRACTEATUM strawflower	3	July to frost	X	X			X
HELIOPSIS (hybrids) orange sunflower	2–4	June– Sept.	X				
HELIOTROPIUM ARBORESCENS heliotrope, cherry-pie	1½–2½	Summer				X	
HELLEBORUS NIGER Christmas-rose	1–1½	Winter					X
HELLEBORUS ORIENTALIS Lenten-rose	1–1½	Spring		X		X	X
HEMEROCALLIS (various) daylily	1½–5	Summer	X	X	X		X
HESPERIS MATRONALIS sweet-rocket	3	June– Aug.		X		X	X

213

PLANT	Height in feet	Season of bloom	Y	P	R	B	W
HEUCHERA SANGUINEA coralbells	1½–3	June– Aug.		X	X		X
HIBISCUS SYRIACUS mallow, rose-of-Sharon	8–10	July– Aug.		X		X	X
HOSTA (various) plaintain-lily	2–3	Summer				X	XL
HUNNEMANIA FUMARIAEFOLIA Mexican tulip-poppy	1½	July to frost	X				
HYACINTHUS ORIENTALIS hyacinth	1–1½	Spring	X	X		X	X
HYDRANGEA HORTENSIS French hydrangea	3–6	Summer		X		X	X
HYDRANGEA PANICULATA	3–6	Summer					X
HYDRANGEA PETIOLARIS climbing hydrangea	20–30	June					X
HYPERICUM (various) St. John's-wort	1–2	Summer	X				
IBERIS SEMPERVIRENS hardy candytuft	1	May					X
IBERIS UMBELLATA globe candytuft	1	Summer		X		X	X
IMPATIENS BALSAMINA garden balsam, lady-slipper	1–2½	Summer		X	X	X	X
IMPATIENS HOLSTI	½–2	Summer		X	X		X
IMPATIENS SULTANI busy-Lizzie	½–2	Summer		X	X		
IPOMEA PURPUREA morning-glory	15	Summer		X		X	X
IPOMOEA NOCTIFLORA moonflower	10	Aug.– Sept.					X
IRIS (various)	½–4	Spring or summer	X	X		X	X
ISMENE CALATHINA Peruvian-daffodil	1½–2	Early summer					X

PLANT	Height in feet	Season of bloom	Y	P	R	B	W
KALMIA LATIFOLIA mountain-laurel	2–6	May– June		X			
KNIPHOFIA (hybrids) poker-plant, torch-lily	3	June to frost	X	X	X		X
KOLKWITZIA AMABILIS beauty-bush	6–8	June		X			
LABURNUM VOSSI goldenchain-tree	30	May– June	X				
LAGERSTROEMIA INDICA crape-myrtle	10–20	Summer		X			X
LATHYRUS ODORATUS sweet pea	2–6	Early summer		X	X	X	X
LAVANDULA OFFICINALIS lavender	1½–2	July– Aug.				X	
LEUCOJUM VERNUM snowflake	to 1	Early spring					X
LIATRIS (various) gayfeather	3–5	Late summer		X		X	X
LILIUM (various)	1½–5	Various	X	X	X		X
LILIUM 'Pink Glory' strain	2½–3	July– Aug.		X			
LIMONIUM LATIFOLIUM sea-lavender	1–2½	July to frost		X		X	X
LIMONIUM SINUATUM statice	1–1½	July to frost	X			X	X
LINUM PERENNE blue flax	1–1½	June– July				X	X
LOBELIA CARDINALIS cardinal-flower	3–4	Mid- summer			X		
LOBELIA ERINUS lobelia	under 1	Summer		X		X	X
LOBULARIA MARITIMA sweet-alyssum	under 1	Summer		X		X	X
LONICERA (various) honeysuckle	6–20	Summer	X				X

PLANT	Height in feet	Season of bloom	Y	P	R	B	W
LUNARIA BIENNIS honesty, money-plant	2–3	(seed-pods)					XF
LUPINUS POLYPHYLLUS lupine	2–3	June	X	X		X	X
LYCHNIS CHALCEDONICA Maltese cross	2–4	June–July		X	X		X
LYTHRUM (hybrids) loosestrife	3–6	July–Sept.		X		X	
MAGNOLIA (various)	6–20	Spring		X		X	X
MAHONIA AQUIFOLIUM Oregon holly-grape	2–5	May	X			XF	
MALUS (various) flowering crabapple	10–30	Apr.–May		X	XF		X
MATHIOLA INCANA stock	1–2	Summer	X	X		X	X
MATRICARIA EXIMIA feverfew	1–2	Summer	X				X
MERTENSIA VIRGINICA Virginia bluebells	1–2	Spring				X	
MIRABILIS JALAPA four-o'clock	1½–2½	Aug.–Oct.	X	X	X	X	X
MOLUCELLA LAEVIS bells-of-Ireland	2–3	Summer					G
MONARDA DIDYMA bergamot, beebalm	3–5	July		X	X	X	X
MUSCARI (various) grape-hyacinth	under 1	Spring		X		X	X
MYOSOTIS ALPESTRIS forget-me-not	½	May				X	
MYOSOTIS PALUSTRIS forget-me-not	to 1	Summer				X	
NARCISSUS (various) daffodil	1–1½	Spring	X	X			X
NEMESIA STRUMOSA figwort	to 1	Summer	X	X	X		X
NEPETA MUSSINI catmint	1–1½	June				X	

216

PLANT	Height in feet	Season of bloom	Y	P	R	B	W
NICOTIANA ALATA ornamental tobacco	2½–4	Summer		X	X	X	XG
NIEREMBERGIA CAERULEA cup-flower	under 1	Mid-summer				X	
NIGELLA DAMASCENA love-in-a-mist	1½	July–Aug.		X		X	
OCIMUM BASILICUM sweet basil	2	Summer		X	XL		
OENOTHERA FRUTICOSA evening-primrose, sundrops	1–2	June–July	X				
ORNITHOGALUM UMBELLATUM star-of-Bethlehem	under 1	Late spring					X
OXYDENDRUM ARBOREUM sorrel-tree, sourwood	15–30	July					X
PAEONIA ALBIFLORA herbaceous	3–5	May–June		X			X
PAEONIA SUFFRUTICOSA tree peony	3–6	Early May	X	X			X
PAPAVER ORIENTALE Oriental poppy	2–3	May–June	X	X	X	X	X
PAPAVER RHOEAS Shirley poppy	2½–3	May–June		X	X		
PELARGONIUM (various) geranium	to 1½	Summer		X	X		X
PENSTEMON (hybrids) beard-tongue	2–4	June–Aug.		X	X	X	X
PETUNIA HYBRIDA	1–2	Summer	X	X	X	X	X
PHILADELPHUS LEMOINEI mock-orange	3–6	June					X
PHLOX DECUSSATA hardy garden phlox	½–4	July–Aug.		X	X	X	X
PHLOX DIVARICATA wild sweet-William	1½	Spring				X	
PHLOX DRUMMONDI annual phlox	½–1½	July to frost	X	X		X	X
PHLOX SUBULATA mountain-pink, creeping phlox	under 1	Spring		X		X	X

PLANT	Height in feet	Season of bloom	Y	P	R	B	W
PHYSOSTEGIA VIRGINIANA false-dragonhead	2–4	July– Aug.		X		X	X
PLATYCODON GRANDIFLORUM balloon-flower	1–3	July				X	X
POLYGONUM AUBERTI silver-lace-vine	15–20	Aug.– Sept.					X
POLYGONUM ORIENTALE prince's-feather	3–5	July to frost		X			
PORTULACARIA GRANDIFLORA portulaca, rose-moss	under 1	Summer	X	X	X	X	X
POTENTILLA FRUTICOSA buttercup-bush	2–3	June	X		X		
PRIMULA (various) primrose, cowslip, oxlip	½–1	Spring	X	X		X	X
PRUNUS (various) flowering cherry, almond, plum	3–20	Spring		X	XF		X
PULMONARIA (hybrids) lungwort	under 1	Spring				X	
PUSCHKINIA SCILLOIDES striped squill	½	Spring					X
PYRACANTHA COCCINEA LALANDI firethorn	6	Spring			XF		
RANUNCULUS ASIATICUS Persian buttercup	1	Apr.– May	X	X			X
RHODODENRON (various)	1½–15	Spring– summer		X	X	X	X
ROSA (various) rose	under 1–10	Summer	X	X	X		X
RUDBECKIA HIRTA black-eyed Susan, coneflower	3–4	Summer	X				
RUDBECKIA (hybrids) gloriosa daisy	1½–5	Late summer	X		X		
RUTA GRAVEOLENS herb-of-grace, rue	1½–2	(leaves)					XL
SALPIGLOSSIS SINUATA painted-tongue	2–3	Summer	X	X		X	
SALVIA FARINACEA blue sage	1–3	Summer		X		X	

PLANT	Height in feet	Season of bloom	Y	P	R	B	W
SALVIA SPLENDENS .... scarlet sage	1–3	Summer to frost			X		
SCABIOSA ATROPURPUREA .... pincushion-flower	1–2	Summer	X	X		X	X
SCILLA SIBIRICA .... Siberian squill	to 1	April		X		X	X
SCILLA HISPANICA	to 1	May– June		X		X	X
SEDUM (various) .... stonecrop, live forever	to 1	Summer	X	X			
SEMPERVIVUM (various) .... hen-and-chickens, houseleek	under 1	(leaves)					XL
SIDALCEA MALVAEFLORA .... checker-bloom	1½–2	July– Sept.		X			
SPIREA (various) .... bridal-wreath	3–6	Spring		X			X
SPREKELIA FORMOSISSIMA .... Aztec-lily, St. James-lily	1–2	Summer			X		
STACHYS LANATA .... betony, lamb's-ears	under 1	(leaves)					XL
STOKESIA LAEVIS .... Stoke's-aster	1–1½	Summer		X		X	X
SYRINGA VULGARIS .... lilac	6–8	May– June		X		X	X
TAGETES (various) .... marigold	½–4	Summer	X				
TALINUM PANICULATUM .... jewels of Opar	2	June– July		X			
TAMARIX (hybrids) .... tamarisk	6	Late summer		X			
THUNBERGIA ALATA .... black-eyed-Susan-vine	5	Summer	X				
THYMUS (various) .... decorative thyme	under 1	June		X		X	X
TIGRIDIA PAVONIA .... Mexican shell-flower	2–3	Summer	X		X		X
TITHONIA ROTUNDIFOLIA .... Mexican sunflower	4–6	July to frost	X				

PLANT	Height in feet	Season of bloom	Y	P	R	B	W
TORENIA FOURNIERI wishbone-flower	up to 1	Summer				X	
TRADESCANTIA VIRGINIANA spiderwort	1–1½	June–July				X	X
TRILLIUM GRANDIFLORUM wake-robin	1½	Spring		X	X		X
TROPAEOLUM MAJUS nasturtium	1	July to frost	X		X		
TULIPA (various) tulip	½–3	Spring	X	X	X	X	X
VALERIANA OFFICINALIS garden-heliotrope	3–5	June		X		G	X
VERBENA HORTENSIS garden verbena	1–1½	Summer		X		X	X
VERONICA INCANA speedwell	½–3	June–July				X	X
VIBURNUM (various)	4–12	May–June		X	XF		X
VINCA MINOR myrtle	½	May–June				X	X
VINCA ROSEA Madagascar periwinkle	under 1–1½	Summer		X	X		X
VIOLA CORNUTA (hybrids) tufted pansy, viola	½	Spring	X			X	X
VIOLA ODORATA sweet violet	½	Spring		X		X	X
VIOLA TRICOLOR HORTENSIS pansy	under 1	Spring	X			X	X
VITEX MACROPHYLLA chaste-tree	6–10	July–Aug.				X	X
WEIGELA (various)	3–6	May–June		X	X		
WISTERIA (various)	12–40	May		X		X	X
YUCCA FILAMENTOSA Adam's-needle	4–6	July					X
ZANTEDESCHIA (various) calla-lily	2–3	Summer	X	X			X
ZINNIA (hybrids)	1–4	Summer	X	X	X		G

Sources of Plants and Seeds

MUCH of the plant material described in this book may be purchased by mail-order from one or more of the nurseries listed below. These firms usually have catalogs available for the asking or for a small charge to help defray printing costs. Exclusively wholesale growers are not listed, for obvious reasons; but gardeners owe a great debt to them, since it is they —and some of the retailers as well—who develop and distribute the fine new hybrids and varieties. Local nurseries and some garden centers also carry many of the better-known plants.

Of course the list is far from complete, comprising only seedsmen and plantsmen with whom I have had dealings and from whom you may expect quality merchandise and good service. There are many other excellent firms in virtually all states.

"The Plant Buyer's Guide" published by the Massachusetts Horticultural Society (Boston) lists a great number of plants by genus, species, and form, each one being keyed to an index of nurserymen and seedsmen who offer it. For obtaining unusual plants this is an invaluable reference book. It is revised and brought up to date from time to time.

American Perennial Gardens
Box 37
Garden City, Mich.   48135

Perennial plants and seeds

Breck's of Boston
200 Breck Building
Boston, Mass.   02210

Plants, bulbs, seeds

Bristol Nurseries
Bristol, Conn.   06010

Garden chrysanthemums

Burgess Seed & Plant Co. Galesburg, Mich. 49053	Trees, shrubs, perennials, seeds
Burnett Bros., Inc. 92 Chambers St. New York, N.Y. 10007	Flower and vegetable seeds
W. Atlee Burpee Co. Philadelphia, Pa. 19132	Bulbs, seeds
The Conard-Pyle Company West Grove, Pa. 19390	"Star Roses"
Cooley's Gardens Silverton, Ore. 97381	Iris
P. deJager & Sons, Inc. 188 Asbury Street South Hamilton, Mass. 01982	Bulb specialties, iris
Earle Dilatush Holly Nursery Robbinsville, N.J. 08691	Hybrid hollies
Eisler Nurseries Box 70 Butler, Pa. 16001	Trees, shrubs
Henry Field Seed & Nursery Co. 19 N. 12th St. Shenandoah, Iowa 51601	Trees, shrubs, bulbs, seeds
James I. George & Son Box 30 Fairport, N.Y. 14450	Clematis
Girard Nurseries Geneva, Ohio 44041	Trees, shrubs
Joseph Harris Company, Inc. 32 Moreton Farm Rochester, N.Y. 14624	Seeds

Inter-State Nurseries, Inc.　　　Trees, shrubs, perennials, bulbs
Hamburg, Iowa   51640

Jackson & Perkins Co.　　　Roses, perennials
1 Rose Lane
Medford, Ore.   97501

Kelly Bros. Nurseries, Inc.　　　Trees, shrubs
Dansville, N.Y.   14437

The Kilgore Seed Company　　　Vegetable and flower seeds
Division of Asgrow Seed Co.
Plant City, Fla.   33566

A. Ladygo Nursery　　　Chrysanthemums
Box 597
Tryon, N.C.   28782

Lamb Nurseries　　　Perennials
E. 101 Sharp Ave.
Spokane, Wash.   99202

Leslie's Wild Flower Nursery　　　Wild flowers, seeds, and plants
30 Summer Street
Methuen, Mass.   01844

Walter Marx Gardens　　　Iris, perennials, bulbs
Boring, Ore.   97009

Early May Seed & Nursery Co.　　　Seeds
9049 Elm Street
Shenandoah, Iowa   51601

Mayfair Nurseries　　　Dwarf conifers, heaths, shrubs,
R.D.2　　　odd and rare plants
Nichols, N.Y.   13812

Mellinger's　　　Trees, shrubs
North Lima 8, Ohio   44452

The Merrys　　　Daylilies, iris, chrysanthemums
109 Brookside Road
Needham, Mass.   02192

Oliver Nurseries 1159 Bronson Road Fairfield, Conn. 06430	Azaleas, rhododendrons
Oregon Bulb Farms Box 529 Gresham, Ore. 97030	Lilies exclusively
George W. Park Seed Co., Inc. Greenwood, S.C. 29646	Seeds, plants, bulbs
Prairie Gem Ranch Smithwick, S.D. 47782	Perennial seeds
Putney Nursery, Inc. Putney, Vt. 05346	Wildflower and perennial plants
Rainbow Hybridizing Gardens 2036 Carson Road Placerville, Calif. 95667	Iris
Rakestraw's Gardens G 3094 S. Term Flint, Mich. 48507	Rock garden plants
Rex Bulb Farms Box 145-F. Newberg, Ore. 97132	Lilies
River's Edge Flower Farm Route 3 Gloucester, Va. 23061	Daffodils, tulips, hyacinths
Robson Quality Seeds, Inc. Hall, N.Y. 14463	Seeds
Rogers Flowers Lexington, S.C. 29072	Chrysanthemums
Russell Gardens Spring, Tex. 77373	Daylilies

Harry E. Saier   Seeds
Dimondale, Mich.   48821

Schreiner's Gardens   Iris, daylilies
3625 Quinaby Road, N.E.
Route 2
Salem, Ore.   97303

R. H. Shumway   Seeds
Rockford, Ill.   61101

Siskiyou Rare Plant Nursery   Alpine and rock garden plants
522 Franquette St.
Medford, Ore.   97501

Sky-Cleft Gardens   Perennials, wildflowers, ferns, herbs
Camp Street Extension
Barre, Vt.   05641

Southern Meadows Garden   Iris, daylilies
Box 230
Centralia, Ill.   62801

Spring Hill Nurseries   Trees, shrubs, perennials
Tipp City, Ohio   45371

Stern's Nurseries, Inc.   Trees, shrubs, perennials
Geneva, N.Y.   14456

Sunnyslope Gardens   Chrysanthemums
8638 Huntington Drive
San Gabriel, Calif.   91775

Talmadge's Fern Gardens   Ferns
354 "G" Street
Chula Vista, Calif.   92010

Thon's Garden Mums   Chrysanthemums
4815 Oak St.
Crystal Lake, Ill.   60014

Van Bourgondien Bros. Farmingdale Road, Route 109 Box A, Babylon, N.Y. 11702	Bulbs
Marinus Van der Pol Washington St. Fairhaven, Mass. 02719	Clematis
Vetterle & Reinelt Capitola, Calif. 95010	Plants and seed of delphinium, tuberous begonias, primulas
The Wayside Gardens Co. Mentor, Ohio 44060	Trees, shrubs, roses, hardy plants, bulbs
White Flower Farm Litchfield, Conn. 06759	Trees, shrubs, perennials
Gilbert H. Wild & Son, Inc. Sarcoxie, Mo. 64862	Peonies, iris, daylilies
Melvin E. Wyant, Rose Specialist, Inc. 200 Johnny Cake Ridge Mentor, Ohio 44060	Roses

Index

ABOUT THE AUTHOR

Elda Haring is a dedicated gardener and has been for many years. Her present garden, now some fifteen years old, is in Greenwich, Connecticut. Here she has grown the plants described in this book and in *The Complete Book of Growing Plants from Seed,* and many more as well. Her handsome perennial border—350 feet long and 8 feet wide—follows the seasons and is so well planned that it is always full of color. Her husband shares her enthusiasm and, with his camera, records the beauties of the plantings they have made together.

Born in Baltimore, Maryland, and educated at Florida State University, the author is a member of the Garden Writers Association of America, the American Begonia Society, the American Gesneriad Society, the National Chrysanthemum Society, the American Horticultural Society, and her own Green Acres Garden Club in Armonk, New York. She is a life member of the Federated Garden Clubs of New York State and a writer for their *News.* She is also active in the local Greenwich Garden Center. Mrs. Haring lectures and writes on horticultural subjects and has contributed articles to *The Begonian, The Floral Magazine, Flower and Garden, Indoor Light Gardening,* and the garden pages of *The New York Times.*